# Dancing with Islam's Assassins

*This Book Could Save Your Life!*

## Chris Panos

Gold International Books Inc.
Houston

**ISBN 0-910743-11-8**
Second Edition
First Printing
Printed in the United State of America

# Dedication

This book is dedicated to the families of America

# Table of Contents

# FOREWORD

You won't get very far into this book without finding out that we are in a war and the Arabs are our enemies. However, in Matthew 5:44 Jesus said, "But I say unto you, Love your enemies, bless them that curse you, do good to them that hate you, and pray for them which despitefully use you, and persecute you." So no matter what you read in the coming pages about Islam's assassins, suicide bombers, radical Islam, and jihadists, please be assured that I love the Arabs—and so does God. And so should you.

How do I know God loves the Arabs? The Bible tells us that Abraham had two sons: Ishmael, Abraham's firstborn, who became the father of the Arabs, and Isaac, who became the father of the Jews. Both peoples were blessed by God. In Genesis 17:20, God told Abraham, "And as for Ishmael, I have heard thee: Behold, I have blessed him, and will make him fruitful, and will multiply him exceedingly; twelve princes shall he beget, and I will make him a great nation."

God made a special covenant with Isaac, but Ishmael also received a blessing. The interesting thing about this is that the blessings of God are irrevocable. There was a time when a king named Balak wanted a prophet named Balaam to curse the Jews. Balaam explained, "God *is* not a man, that he should lie; neither the son of man, that he should repent: hath he said, and shall he not do *it*? or hath he spoken, and shall he not make it good? Behold, I have received *commandment* to bless: and he hath blessed; and I cannot reverse it" (Numbers 23:19-20).

In New Testament times, the Jews persecuted the early Christians, yet Paul told the Romans they were still beloved by God: "As concerning the gospel, *they are* enemies for your sakes: but as touching the election, *they are* beloved for the fathers' sakes. For the gifts and calling of God *are* without repentance (Romans 11:28-29). The New Living Translation translates "without repentance" as "can never be withdrawn."

The King James Bible tells us that "God is no respecter of persons" (Acts 10:24). In modern English, "God does not play favorites." If the Jews' blessing is irrevocable, then so is the Arabs'. Eventually, there will come a time when the animosity between the Jews and the Arabs will be healed: "In that day shall Israel be the third with Egypt and with Assyria, *even* a blessing in the midst of the land: Whom the LORD of hosts shall bless, saying, Blessed *be* Egypt my people, and Assyria the work of my hands, and Israel mine inheritance." (Isaiah 19:24-25).

I believe that every person is made in the image of God. Every person can be saved, no matter what his religious background and no matter what atrocities he has committed. If you are a militant Muslim, and you are reading this book, God loves you. He doesn't want you to go to hell. He doesn't care how many people you may have murdered. He doesn't care what sins you have committed. God doesn't want *anyone* to go to hell. That's why the Bible says, "The Lord is not slack concerning his promise, as some men count slackness; but is longsuffering to us-ward, not willing that any should perish, but that all should come to repentance" (2 Peter 3:9). It also says, "And it shall come to pass, *that* whosoever shall call on the name of the Lord shall be saved" (Acts 2:21).

You are "whosoever" and the name of the Lord is "Jesus." The Bible says, "Therefore let all the house of Israel know assuredly, that God hath made that same Jesus, whom ye have crucified, both Lord and Christ" (Acts 2:36).

I have been told that Muslims revere Jesus as a prophet. If He was a prophet, then He must have been speaking the truth when He said (to the unbelieving) "I said therefore unto you, that ye shall die in your sins: for if ye believe not that I am *he*, ye shall die in your sins" (John 8:24).

It is my heartfelt prayer that everyone who reads even a part of this book will be saved from dying in sin and going to hell. If you would like to be saved right now, please turn immediately to Page 261, "Six Scriptural Steps to Salvation." The rest of this book will be waiting after you are born again.

# INTRODUCTION

Islamic fundamentalists—Muslim terrorists—are a threat to the safety and security of all non-Muslims. Nobody is surprised to find out that Muslims hate the Jews. What has come as a shock until comparatively recently is that Muslims hate *all* non-Muslims, especially Westerners, and especially Americans.

In a statement attributed to John Negroponte, director of national intelligence, the *Wall Street Journal* tells us that "Islamist terrorism, especially from al Qaeda, remains the chief national security threat to the US in a world where components of weapons of mass destruction are increasingly abundant."[1]

Islamic terrorism impacts everybody, Muslim and non-Muslim alike. If you are a Sunni Muslim, you need to worry about Shiite Muslims; if you are a Shiite Muslim, you need to worry about the Sunnis. Do you live in a country that has a secular Muslim government? Muslim extremists do not believe in the separation of church and state. Muslim extremists would like to overthrow all secular Muslim governments and replace them with a theocracy that would be governed by Muslim law. Muslim extremists do not mind killing Muslim civilians in the course of waging a jihad. They will impose their own strict interpretations of Islamic religious law as the law of the land in any country if they can. Their goal is an all-Muslim world ruled by strict Muslim law.

The first part of this book discusses Islamic terrorists: what they believe, and what they plan to do. It discusses Muslim disinformation—how Muslims use the press to plant the lies that will further their cause. It discusses the weapons of mass destruction that are available to Islamist terrorists now. And it gives you just enough historical background so you can see how we arrived where we are today.

Part Two discusses Islamic terrorism and the times we live in from a Biblical perspective. Islamic terrorists and their nuclear, biological, and chemical weapons of mass destruction are a major threat to world peace. But terrorists are not the only threat to human health and wellbeing. We live in a time when the very forces of nature—earthquakes, tsunamis, hurricanes, epidemics and disturbances in the heavenlies—will cause "distress of nations, with perplexity." Part Two includes a discussion of these additional threats as well.

Part Three tells you what you can do now to increase your chances of surviving the times we live in—steps you can take to protect yourself and your family in the case of chemical, biochemical and nuclear warfare, as well as natural disaster. Of course all of us know that there isn't much you can do if you're standing at Ground Zero when a nuclear bomb is dropped. There are, however, a number of things you can do to increase your chances of surviving terrorist attacks and other emergencies. In the next terrorist attack on US soil, not all of us will be at Ground Zero. Some of us will be located where survival is possible if certain steps are taken. These steps are outlined in Part Three.

*PART 1—AN INTRODUCTION TO RADICAL ISLAM*

*"**Chris Panos** shared his views on the current state of Islam, and how it conflicts with the West. Having spent decades working with Muslims all over the world, he's come to believe that the Islamic mindset involves world domination.*
*Specifically, he said Iran's leader, Pres. Ahmadinejad is a greater threat than bin Laden. Panos suggested that military action be taken against Iran, arguing that the country could be "put out of business" in just "seven days." Such action would reduce the possibility of nuclear devices being smuggled in the U.S., he said."*
George Noory, host of Coast To Coast.com

# CHAPTER 1

# UPDATE 2007

Eccelesiastes 3:8 tells us there is "A time to love, and a time to hate; a time of war, and a time of peace." Unfortunately, we are living in a time of war. I recently had the opportunity to appear on George Noory's program, *Coast to Coast.com* and share my belief that decisive military action should be taken against Iran. I believe that the United States must take action against Iran before Iran takes action against us.

The United States Department of State regards Iran as the world's foremost state sponsor of terrorism, as spelled out in the following paragraph:

> Iran remained the most active state sponsor of terrorism. Its Islamic Revolutionary Guard Corps (IRGC) and Ministry of Intelligence and Security (MOIS) were directly involved in the planning and support of terrorist acts and continued to exhort a variety of groups, especially Palestinian groups with leadership cadres in Syria and Lebanese Hizballah, to use terrorism in pursuit of their goals. In addition, the IRGC was increasingly involved in supplying lethal assistance to Iraqi militant groups, which destabilizes Iraq.[2]

In January 2007, Iran's President Mahmoud Ahmadinejad was reported as saying that "the United States and the Zionist regime of Israel will soon come to the end of their lives."[3] It was not the first time he had made statements of this nature. As you will read later in this book, there is considerable evidence that Iran is working on a nuclear weapon of its own. Meanwhile, Russian Cold War-era suitcase bombs—portable nuclear devices—are unaccounted for and could be used by Iranian-supported terrorists on US soil.

In the year since *Dancing with Islam's Assassins* went to press with its first edition, things have only gotten worse. This second edition, which will hit the bookstores in September 2007, is actually being revised in July. Here are a few of the developments reported just this month:

## Terrorism

*The Wall Street Journal* reported that "Al Qaeda is stepping up its efforts to sneak terror operatives into the U.S. and has acquired most of the capabilities it needs to strike here, according to a new U.S. intelligence assessment."[4] According to this article:

• Al Qaeda is probably still pursuing chemical, biological or nuclear weapons and would use them if its operatives developed sufficient capability.

• The terror group has been able to restore three of the four key tools it would need to launch an attack on U.S. soil: a safe haven in Pakistan's tribal areas, operational lieutenants and senior leaders. It could not immediately be learned what the missing fourth element is.

• The group will bolster its efforts to position operatives inside U.S. borders. In public statements, U.S. officials have expressed concern about the ease with which people can enter the U.S. through Europe because of a program that allows most Europeans to enter without visas.

The document also discusses increasing concern about individuals already inside the U.S. who are adopting an extremist brand of Islam.

# Iran

On July 9, Reuters reported that Iran is building a new tunnel complex inside a mountain near their Natanz nuclear plant, where uranium is being enriched despite two UN sanctions.[5] According Reuters, nuclear analysts said this was a possible attempt to protect uranium enrichment activity from nuclear attack. The tunnel facility could also be used for defensive weapons including antiaircraft batteries. Commercial satellite imagery from Digital Globe showed the tunnel complex on June 11, but was not apparent in January photos.

# The United Kingdom

At the end of June, two car bombs failed to explode in London and a Jeep Cherokee was rammed into the entrance of Glasgow Airport. At least one of the suspects was a medical doctor of Iranian-Kurdish background. On July 2, former Scotland Yard police chief Sir John Stevens was quoted in *The New York Times* as saying that the car bombs signaled "a major escalation in the war being waged on us by Islamic terrorists." According to him, "It is not simply the horror of yet more attempts at mass murder that is so chilling -- but the change in the psychotic thought processes behind it....Now it is clear a loose but deadly network of interlinked operational cells has developed. Al Qaeda has imported the tactics of Baghdad and Bali onto the streets of the U.K.,' he said."[6]

If Al Qaeda has imported terrorist tactics into the UK, what is to stop them from importing the same tactics into the US?

## Israel

Meanwhile, the Middle East is a powder keg. The threat level to the nation of Israel is extreme. A July 2007 article in The Jerusalem Post reports it this way:

> The red telephone next to his bed wakes up Military Intelligence head Maj.-Gen. Amos Yadlin on almost a nightly basis. Since 1973, the country has not faced such a large number of threats - all equal in their level of danger - as today. When Yadlin's phone rings in the middle of the night, the call could be related to one of five different fronts. It could be a call about changes in Syrian military formation, indicating that war is imminent; developments in Iran's nuclear program; Hizbullah plans to kidnap a soldier; a Hamas attack in the Gaza Strip; or Global Jihad plans to hijack a plane and ram it in to the Azrieli Towers in Tel Aviv. ...

> According to Military Intelligence's up-to-date assessments, obtained this week by The Jerusalem Post, the country is heading toward a number of major military conflicts in the coming year, possibly even in the next few months.

> Hizbullah is rearming and, according to the IDF, is back at the level of strength it possessed before the war.

Syria is in the midst of an unprecedented weapons shopping spree and making final preparations for war.

Iran is racing toward nuclear power and, if not stopped, might obtain a nuke by as early as 2009.

Hamas has established an enemy Islamic state five minutes south of Ashkelon.

And al-Qaida has declared Israel as one of its primary targets for the coming year.[7]

# Lebanon

As of this writing, Al-Qaeda-inspired militants have been barricaded inside the Nahr al-Bared Palestinian refugee camp in Lebanon since May 20. At least 219 people have died in Lebanon's worst internal violence since their 1975-1890 civil war. According to Reuters, "Lebanese troops pounded a Palestinian refugee camp in north Lebanon on Saturday [July 14] where barricaded al Qaeda-inspired militants fired eight Katyusha-type rockets, a military source said. The army and Fatah al-Islam militants have fought often ferocious battles at the coastal Nahr al-Bared refugee camp for nearly eight weeks with no sign the Islamist militants will heed calls to surrender."[8]

# Turkey

According to Reuters, Turkey, which shares part of its southern border with Iraq, has boosted its troop levels there to over 200,000. According to this article, "The unusually large-scale buildup, which includes tanks, heavy artillery and aircraft, is part of a security crackdown on Kurdish rebels hiding in southeast Turkey and northern Iraq... NATO member Turkey has refused to rule out a possible cross-border operation to crush Kurdistan Workers Party (PKK) rebels, despite opposition from the United States and Iraq."[9]

## Russia

Vladimir Putin has signed a decree suspending Russia's role in the Conventional Forces In Europe (CFE) treaty, a pact adopted in 1990 that limits the number of combat aircraft, tanks, and heavy artillery deployed and stored between the Atlantic and the Ural mountains. Both Britain and NATO consider this treaty a "cornerstone" of European security.[10] According to Reuters:

> "Russian threats have materialized and I don't exclude that more steps could follow," said Yevgeny Volk, the head of the Washington-based Heritage Foundation think-tank.
>
> "If there is no agreement with the United States on the missile shield... Russia could potentially go ahead with its threats to retarget (at Europe) and redeploy missiles."[11]

## Where is America in Bible Prophecy?

For a book that foretells the future in great detail, the Bible is strangely silent about the United States during the events of the end times. We can only guess at the reason for this. Some have said that the United States is referred to in the Bible as one of the "young lions of Tarshish." According to *The American Tract Society Dictionary,* "Tarshish may be used as a general expression, applicable to all the distant shores of Europe." If so, Tarshish would include England, whose emblem is a lion; and the United States and other countries that were once part of the British Empire, could conceivably be the "young lions."

There are other possibilities, of course—some better, and some worse. The best-case scenario is that so many United States citizens have been caught up in the Rapture that the few who are left are of little importance on the world stage. If a large-scale end-times revival hits America, as I believe it will, this scenario is entirely possible.

Unfortunately, there are also a couple of possible worst-case scenarios that might explain why America isn't mentioned: one is that the U.S. has been nuked out of existence before the end-time events occur, and the other is that the United States has become part of the Antichrist's one-world government. This latter scenario also strikes me as highly likely.

I hope and pray that I am wrong about this, but current events seem to indicate that the United States could become part of the one-world government that will be headed by the Antichrist. If so, of course the Bible wouldn't mention it as a separate nation—it wouldn't *be* a separate nation.

## The United States of North America?

In March 2005, the elected leaders of Canada, Mexico and the United States announced the establishment of the Security and Prosperity Partnership of North America. This announcement said in part that "Our Partnership is committed to reach the highest results to advance the security and well-being of our people. The Partnership is trilateral in concept; while allowing any two countries to move forward on an issue, it will create a path for the third to join later."[12]

On October 30, 2006, Representative Ron Paul, R-Texas, denounced plans for the proposed Nafta Superhighway as part of a larger plot to merge the United States, Canada, and Mexico into a North American Union. He said the ultimate goal of the superhighway was actually "an integrated North American Union – complete with a currency, a cross-national bureaucracy and virtually borderless travel within the union. Like the European Union, a North American Union would represent another step toward the abolition of national sovereignty altogether."[13]

On the very next day—October 31, 2006—Enrique Berruga, Mexico's ambassador to the United Nations, explicitly stated that a North American Union is needed—and even said that it needed to be complete within the next eight years because of the coming wave of U.S. baby boomer retirees.[14]

Shortly thereafter, in a November 2006 interview, Representative Tom Tancredo, R-Colorado, told *WorldNetDaily* that "President Bush believes America should be more of an idea than an actual place." *WorldNetDaily* quoted Tom Tancredo as saying that "I know this is dramatic – or maybe somebody would say overly dramatic – but I'm telling you, that everything I see leads me to believe that this whole idea of the North American Union, it's not something that just is written about by right-wing fringe kooks. It is something in the head of the president of the United States, the president of Mexico, I think the prime minister of Canada buys into it…"[15]

Commentators see these developments as possibly going even further, into a Union of the Americas. According to Online Journal Associate Editor Jerry Mazza, "The establishment of a Union of the Americas is the longed for wish of the neocon colonizers and their current enabler, George W. Bush. It is to be accomplished with the help of the North American Union (with Canada), Clinton's NAFTA (North American Free Trade Agreement) and Bush's own CAFTA (Central American Free Trade Agreement). The idea is to mix the United States, North and eventually South Americas into one banquet for the multi-national corporations to gobble."[16]

If the United States heads in this direction—and again, I hope and pray it doesn't—then it's not too farfetched to see an eventual merger of a future Union of the Americas with the European Union under the leadership of the Antichrist.

## The European Union and Seat Number 666

Meanwhile, what are we to think of the European Union? In an article in the *Free Republic*, Ian Paisley points out that the symbol chosen by the European Union is the Woman riding the Beast. "This comes from a prophecy in Revelation 17," Paisley writes. "The depiction of the harlot woman was reproduced on the centenary stamp of the European Union, in a huge painting in the

Parliament's new building in Brussels, and by a huge sculpture outside the new E.U. Council of Ministers Office in Brussels. The new European coinage, the Euro, bears the same insignia. The Tower of Babel has been used on the posters emanating from Europe... a truly suggestive prophetic sign."[17]

According to another prophetic website, "The EU's 'Parliament' Building in Strasbourg has been deliberately designed to represent the Tower of Babel, as per the famous painting by Peter Brueghel, painted in 1563. The logic behind this symbolism is [that] the... EU is seeking to 'build the house of Europe' - a task yet to be completed. The building is complete and in use, but is designed to look unfinished, and even has ringed platforms around it to represent scaffolding. When asked by a secular journalist 'Why the Tower of Babel?' an EU official replied, 'What they failed to complete 3000 years ago – we in Europe will finish now.'"[18]

Paisley's article mentions something even more ominous. Speaking of the parliament building, Paisley writes, "It is certainly a building of the Space Age. The seats of its massive hemicycle are designed like the crew seats in the Star Trek space machines. There are 679 of them – but wait for it! While these seats are allocated to Members, one seat remains unallocated and unoccupied. The number of that seat is 666."

Paisley concludes his article by saying:

> Revelation 13:18: "Here is wisdom. Let him that hath understanding count the number of the beast: for it is the number of a man; and his number is Six hundred threescore and six." That is 666.
>
> Today this scripture is being fulfilled before our very eyes.
>
> The Antichrist's seat will be occupied. The world awaits his full and final development. The Lord will destroy him by the spirit of His mouth (the Word of God) and by the brightness of His coming (2 Thes. 2:8). The coming of the Lord draweth nigh.[19]

The beast is coming. We can't avoid it—it's in the Bible. God said it, and that settles it. As believers, however, it is important for us not to contribute to the beast's arrival or his kingdom just because we know it's inevitable. Jesus said, "Woe unto the world because of offences! for it must needs be that offences come; but woe to that man by whom the offence cometh!" (Matthew 18:7).

What should we do, then? The Bible says it best: "Let us hold fast the profession of *our* faith without wavering; (for he *is* faithful that promised;) And let us consider one another to provoke unto love and to good works: Not forsaking the assembling of ourselves together, as the manner of some *is*; but exhorting *one another*: and so much the more, as ye see the day approaching" (Hebrews 10:23-25).

Beloved, anyone who knows the Bible and reads the news can "see the day approaching." The hour is late. We live in a time when changes can take place very quickly. It is time for Christians to walk uprightly, to love one another and to hold no grudge against anyone. And it is also time to expect a great revival, for according to Isaiah 59:19, "...When the enemy shall come in like a flood, the Spirit of the LORD shall lift up a standard against him."

Paul told Timothy that "in the last days perilous times shall come" (2 Timothy 3:1). What should we Christians be doing as we approach the end of the age? In Mark 13:33-37, Jesus has already told us what we need to do:

> Take ye heed, watch and pray: for ye know not when the time is. For the Son of man is as a man taking a far journey, who left his house, and gave authority to his servants, and to every man his work, and commanded the porter to watch. Watch ye therefore: for ye know not when the master of the house cometh, at even, or at midnight, or at the cockcrowing, or in the morning: Lest coming suddenly he find you sleeping. And what I say unto you I say unto all, Watch.

*"We did not have a revolution in order to have democracy."*[20]
Iranian President Mahmoud Ahmadinejad

# CHAPTER 2

# A MUSLIM ANTICHRIST?

As we went to press with the first edition of this book, a new book was slated to hit the bookstores in Iran. Entitled *Ahmadinejad: the Third Millennium Miracle*, it was written by Fatemeh Rajabi, wife of government spokesman Gholam-Hossein Elham. According to Pakistan's Daily Times, the FardaNews website said that "in her book, Rajabi will express her belief and the reasons to prove Ahmadinejad is a third millennium miracle on earth."[21]

On February 13, 2006, *Newsweek* magazine ran a cover story that asked, "How Dangerous is Ahmadinejad?" As a secular magazine, Newsweek didn't think to ask whether Ahmadinejad was the Antichrist or not.

If Ahmadinejad *is* the Antichrist, then when Newsweek asks "How dangerous is Ahmadinejad" we can wholeheartedly answer, "Very dangerous indeed."

Those of us who come from the Bible Belt know what "Antichrist" means. For those of you who don't, the word "Antichrist" comes from Greek roots meaning "against" and "Christ." Merriam-Webster defines Antichrist as "one who denies or opposes Christ; specifically: a great antagonist expected to fill the world with wickedness but to be conquered forever by Christ at his second coming."[22] It is the Antichrist who is identified with the Beast of Revelation, the man who will impose the Mark of the Beast on people's right hands or foreheads: "And he causeth all, both small and great, rich and poor, free and bond, to receive a

27

mark in their right hand, or in their foreheads: And that no man might buy or sell, save he that had the mark, or the name of the beast, or the number of his name" (Revelation 13:16-17).

For Christians, the terrifying thing about the Antichrist is that receiving the Mark of the Beast is a one-way ticket to Hell: "If any man worship the beast and his image, and receive his mark in his forehead, or in his hand, The same shall drink of the wine of the wrath of God, which is poured out without mixture into the cup of his indignation; and he shall be tormented with fire and brimstone in the presence of the holy angels, and in the presence of the Lamb" (Revelation 14:9-10). Talk about a fate worse than death!

Traditionally, Christians have been taught that the Antichrist would come from Europe, because Bible prophecy indicates that the Antichrist will come from one of the lands of the old Roman Empire. In recent centuries, the world has been ruled by Western nations. We have become so accustomed to a world that is ruled by Western nations that we have forgotten that the old Roman Empire also included the Middle East.

Today, more and more Christians are beginning to wonder whether the Antichrist might not be a Muslim. Some specifically target Ahmadinejad. According to the Tehran *Asia Times Online*, fundamentalist Christians in the United States have "unleashed a ferocious media campaign depicting Iranian President Mahmud Ahmadinejad as the Antichrist who wants to destroy Jerusalem and prevent Jesus' comeback."

What makes Christians think the Antichrist might be a Muslim? For one thing, Christians believe the Lord is coming soon, so of course we expect that the Antichrist will appear in the next few years. If he is going to appear that soon, events in the Middle East make it seem likely that the Antichrist will appear out of Islam. For many, the first clue was that Muslims are known for beheading people. Once upon a time, beheading was very popular, but in this modern day and age, you only hear about beheading by Islamic governments and Islamic terrorists. And we know from the Bible that the Beast will behead people. Revelation 20:4 says:

"And I saw thrones, and they sat upon them, and judgment was given unto them: and I saw the souls of them that were beheaded for the witness of Jesus, and for the word of God, and which had not worshipped the beast, neither his image, neither had received his mark upon their foreheads, or in their hands; and they lived and reigned with Christ a thousand years."

Here are some signs that point to the possibility that the Antichrist will come from a Muslim nation:

| The Antichrist | The Muslims |
|---|---|
| • The Antichrist will behead people | • Muslims already behead people |
| • The Antichrist will head a global government | • Muslims already seek a global government known as a caliphate |
| • The Antichrist will make war with the saints | • Muslims already make war with Christians and Jews |
| • The Antichrist will be the leader of a universal world religion | • Muslims seek to establish a global theocracy |
| • The Antichrist will make war against Israel | • Muslims deny Israel's right to exist |

## Mahmoud Ahmadinejad

Politically, Mahmoud Ahmadinejad can be said to have come out of nowhere. He was appointed mayor of Tehran on May 3, 2003 and elected President on June 24, 2005. He enjoys the full support of Iran's Supreme Leader, Ayatollah Seyyed Ali Khamenei. And, according to Scott Peterson of *The Christian Science Monitor*, he "predicted 'with no doubt' his June election victory, months in advance, at a time when polls gave him barely 1 percent support."[23]

Ahmadinejad is a deeply religious conservative, a

charismatic leader who consorts with terrorists and who is no friend to Israel—and no friend, either, to the United States, which he refers to as "the world oppressor." In October 2005 he caused world outrage by proclaiming that "Israel must be wiped off the map."

> "The establishment of the Zionist regime was a move by the world oppressor against the Islamic world," the president told a conference in Tehran on Wednesday, entitled The World without Zionism.
> "The skirmishes in the occupied land are part of a war of destiny. The outcome of hundreds of years of war will be defined in Palestinian land," he said.
> "As the Imam said, Israel must be wiped off the map," said Ahmadinejad, referring to Iran's revolutionary leader Ayat Allah Khomeini. [24]

According to *ThreatsWatch*, Ahmadinejad went on to tell The World without Zionism Conference that wiping Israel off the map was "very attainable" and would happen "very soon":

> I do not doubt that the new wave which has begun in our dear Palestine and which today we are also witnessing in the Islamic world is a wave of morality which has spread all over the Islamic world. Very soon, this stain of disgrace [i.e. Israel] will vanish from the center of the Islamic world – and this is attainable.[25]

Since that outburst, Ahmadinejad has continued to promote anti-Semitism within Iran. In May 2006, *The New York Times* reported the comments of an Iranian professor as follows: "He is reshaping the identity of the elite," said a political science professor in Tehran who asked not to be identified so as not to affect his relations with government officials. "Being against Jews and Zionists is an essential part of this new identity."[26] Like other anti-Semites, Ahmadinejad denies the Holocaust took place.[27]

According to Al Jazeera, "As a young student, Ahmadinejad

joined an ultraconservative faction of the Office for Strengthening Unity, the radical student group spawned by the 1979 Islamic Revolution, and staged the capture of the US Embassy. According to reports, Ahmadinejad attended planning meetings for the US Embassy takeover..."[28] Although Ahmadinejad denies having been among the hostage-takers, some former US hostages have said that they recognize him as one of their captors. "You could make him a blond and shave his whiskers, put him in a zoot suit and I'd still spot him," said former US hostage Chuck Scott.[29] So Ahmadinejad most likely is a terrorist.

Most troubling of all, Ahmadinejad openly awaits the return of the 12th Imam, a messianic Islamic spiritual leader. In October, he ended a speech to the United Nations General Assembly with the following prayer:

> From the beginning of time, humanity has longed for the day when justice, peace, equality and compassion envelop the world. All of us can contribute to the establishment of such a world. When that day comes, the ultimate promise of all Divine religions will be fulfilled with the emergence of a perfect human being [12th Imam] who is heir to all prophets and pious men. He will lead the world to justice and absolute peace. O mighty Lord, I pray to you to hasten the emergence of your last repository, the promised one, that perfect and pure human being, the one that will fill this world with justice and peace.[30]

In a DVD of Ahmadinejad and Ayatollah Javadi Amoli, Ahmadinejad had this to say about his UN address:

> On the last day when I was speaking, one of our group told me that when I started to say 'Bismillah Muhammad', he saw a green light come from around me, and I was placed inside this aura," he says. "I felt it myself. I felt that the atmosphere suddenly changed, and for those 27 or 28 minutes, all the

leaders of the world did not blink. When I say they
didn't move an eyelid, I'm not exaggerating. They
were looking as if a hand was holding them there,
and had just opened their eyes - Alhamdulillah![31]

Muslims believe that the twelfth descendent of Muhammad,
also known as the Twelfth Imam, or the Mahdi, will be the ultimate
savior of mankind, bringing global peace and justice by establishing
Islam as the world religion. Shiites believe the Mahdi was born in
868 and was subsequently hidden by God until he emerges to fulfill
his mission. Sunnis either believe that the Mahdi has not yet been
born, or that he was born recently and has not yet emerged. Both
Sunnis and Shiites believe that the Mahdi will emerge from Mecca
during the last days of the world, that he and Jesus are two different
individuals, and that the emergence of the Mahdi will precede the
Second Coming of Jesus.

While Muslims differ as to how the Mahdi will emerge,
many Iranian Muslims believe that Allah hid the Mahdi in a well by
the Mosque of Jamkaran in Qom, Iran. Muslims bring their prayer
requests to this well in much the same way as Jews bring theirs to
the Wailing Wall.

According to the UK's *Daily Telegraph*:

> One of the first acts of Mr. Ahmadinejad's
> government was to donate about £10 million to the
> Jamkaran mosque, a popular pilgrimage site where
> the pious come to drop messages to the Hidden
> Imam into a holy well.
>
> All streams of Islam believe in a divine saviour,
> known as the Mahdi, who will appear at the End of
> Days. A common rumour - denied by the
> government but widely believed - is that Mr.
> Ahmadinejad and his cabinet have signed a
> "contract" pledging themselves to work for the
> return of the Mahdi and sent it to Jamkaran.
>
> Iran's dominant "Twelver" sect believes this
> will be Mohammed ibn Hasan, regarded as the 12th

Imam, or righteous descendant of the Prophet Mohammad.

He is said to have gone into "occlusion" in the ninth century, at the age of five. His return will be preceded by cosmic chaos, war and bloodshed. After a cataclysmic confrontation with evil and darkness, the Mahdi will lead the world to an era of universal peace.

This is similar to the Christian vision of the Apocalypse. Indeed, the Hidden Imam is expected to return in the company of Jesus.

Mr Ahmadinejad appears to believe that these events are close at hand and that ordinary mortals can influence the divine timetable.

The prospect of such a man obtaining nuclear weapons is worrying. The unspoken question is this: is Mr Ahmadinejad now tempting a clash with the West because he feels safe in the belief of the imminent return of the Hidden Imam? Worse, might he be trying to provoke chaos in the hope of hastening his reappearance?[32]

As you surely know by now, I myself am a Christian, not a Muslim. My Bible doesn't tell me about a Mahdi, but it does tell me about an Antichrist. When I hear of a messianic figure appearing in the last days—a figure who is not Jesus—then I immediately think "Antichrist." Do I think the Antichrist could appear as the Mahdi? I believe he could. (Most of us believe that the Antichrist will come out of the Roman Empire, but as I've already mentioned, the old Roman Empire also included the Middle East.) Do I think Ahmadinejad is the Antichrist? No, I don't. But I do see him as possibly being a John the Baptist-like forerunner of the Antichrist. And I also see him as "*an* antichrist."

The Apostle John wrote, "Little children, it is the last time: and as ye have heard that antichrist shall come, even now are there many antichrists; whereby we know that it is the last time." (1 John 2:18). The antichrist spirit is loose in the world—and has been since the days of John. Hitler was an antichrist. Stalin was an antichrist. And I firmly believe that Ahmadinejad is an antichrist. But "the" Antichrist? The Bible tells us that "the" Antichrist will be "revealed in his time" (2 Thessalonians 2:6). I believe that time is near. But as of this writing, it hasn't come as yet.

*"Islam seeks the world. It is not satisfied by a piece of land but demands the whole universe."*
Sayyid Abu'l-A'la Mawdudi (1903-1979)

*"And fight them until there is no more polytheism and religion is for Allah alone."*
Surah al-Anfaal

# CHAPTER 3

# THE ISLAMIC TERRORIST MINDSET

## Background—How Muslims See the World

Until September 11, 2001, most Americans lived in a dream world, believing that radical Muslims were mainly a Middle Eastern problem. We knew that "the Muslims" hated Israel. What we didn't realize was how much the Muslims hated us. Taken completely unawares, we wondered who had attacked us and why they hated us so much.

Dr. David Bukay, who teaches in the political science department at the University of Haifa, put it this way: "Only on September 11, 2001, after the terrorist strikes on the Twin Towers and the Pentagon, was the Islamic threat internalized in the West. It then began to penetrate the Western political consciousness that the Arab-Islamic political culture is aggressive and violent, can arouse popular forces that are enormous in scope, and embraces worldwide aspirations."[33]

In an article entitled, "We are All Israelis Now," published on September 18, 2001, Robert Tracinski wrote:

> The terror we experienced last week is what Israelis have lived with for decades, and the motive of the terrorists is the same. Their motive is not

35

solely a hatred for Jews, though that is an important component. Their motive is a wider hatred for the West—for the free, secular society that allows us to flout Islamic law—for the industry, technology, and economic freedom that makes us wealthy—for the military might that makes us invulnerable to conventional attack. The terrorists grasp this commonality, and they hate America, not only because we support Israel, but because Israel shares and represents our values. As a Palestinian cleric declared last year in a sermon at a Gaza mosque—a sermon broadcast on Arafat-controlled television—"Wherever you are, kill the Jews, [and] the Americans, who are like them." This is the enemy against whom we have urged the Israelis to exercise restraint.[34]

Islamic teaching and Islamic law divides the world into two camps: *Dar-al-Islam*, the lands under Islamic control, and *Dar-al-Harb*, the domain or abode of war, which includes any countries *not* under Islamic control. Built into the very language of Islam is the concept that if you are not living in a Muslim land, you are living in *Dar-al-Harb*, the domain or abode of war. *Dar-al-Harb* is in fact a war zone, one where the Muslim rules of war apply, a zone in which non-Muslims are fair game and can expect to be targeted for conquest.

According to Dr. Charles Selengut, professor of sociology and of religious studies at Drew University, "The goal of *jihad* is not to force individual conversion, but the transformation, by forcible conquest if necessary, of non-Muslim areas into Muslim-controlled states, whereby they become part of the Islamic world, the *Dar al-Islam*. Islam, from its earliest periods, permitted monotheistic religions like Christianity and Judaism to maintain their religious institutional life but these communities, known as *dhimmi* communities, while permitting religious and economic rights, were consigned to an inferior status within Muslim society, and subject to special taxes and obligations. Unlike the *dhimmis*, who are tolerated minority communities, citizens of non-Muslim societies are seen as *harbi*, people living in a war zone, and therefore subject to conquest."[35]

A Christian or a Jew living in a Muslim land may be a distinctly second-class citizen, but *theoretically* he is under Muslim protection. A Christian or a Jew living in a *non*-Muslim land is (whether he knows it or not) already at war, and already living in a war zone. Given the opportunity, radical jihadists see it as their duty to conquer the land he lives in.

Thus Muslims believe it is the duty of the faithful to transform non-Muslim lands into Muslim lands and predominantly or secular Muslim lands into lands that are governed by Muslim religious law. The ultimate goal is to turn the whole world into an Islamic theocracy. Forcible conquest is seen as a perfectly acceptable part of this process. It is the religious duty of the Quran-believing, fundamentalist Muslim to wage *jihad* against America— and also, eventually, against *every* non-Muslim nation.

Islamic extremists do not believe in the separation of church and state—that is a Western concept, and a comparatively recent one at that. As used by extremists, the religion of Islam supports the politics of Islam. There are more than 100 verses in the Quran supporting the use of violence in order to spread Islam. Quran 9:5, known as "the verse of the sword, " declares, "Fight and slay the pagans wherever you find them, and seize them, beleaguer them, and lie in wait for them in every stratagem. "

## Why America?

Immediately after September 11, the question on everyone's mind was this: Why America? In his book, *Future Jihad*, Walid Phares answers this question by saying that "the jihadists decided to wage war against the United States simply because it was possible."[36] He goes on to say:

> Throughout history the jihadist ideology aimed
> at taking down *dar el harb*. As long as no reforms

occur in the doctrinal realm, the global objective to defeat what they perceive as the "house of war" will remain standing, for decades or even centuries. My reading of the evolution of the jihadist movement since the beginning of the twentieth century is that by the early 1990s, after the final collapse of the Soviets, the … international network thought that the war against the United States could be won and, more important, that Allah was on the side of the holy warriors.[37]

Why America? America had proved, over and over again, that—up until 9/11 at any rate—we did not take the threat of jihad seriously. In June 1996 a truck bomb exploded outside the Khobar Towers killing 19 American servicemen and wounding hundreds of various nationalities—and we did nothing. In August 1998 car bombs exploded outside US embassies in Nairobi and Dar es Salaam, killing 224 and wounding thousands—and we did nothing. In October 2000, a terrorist bombing killed 17 US soldiers aboard the USS Cole—and we did nothing. Jihadists saw the US as weak and victory as possible. As Walid Phares pointed out, the terrorists attacked because they felt they could.

## Islamist Propaganda

One of the reasons jihad is possible is that for years, Americans has been brainwashed by well-funded Islamist propaganda that plays down militant Islam's intentions. We have been told that terrorism is abhorrent to "true Muslims" and that Islam is actually a peace-loving religion. However, in time of war—and the jihadists do consider themselves to be at war with us—peace is reserved only for other Muslims. (In practice, it turns out that peace is reserved only for other Muslims of a similar Muslim sect.)

Because they consider themselves to be at war with us, radical Muslims feel that they have no obligation to tell Americans the truth about their beliefs or intentions. Years ago, there was a classic advertising slogan that said, "Promise her anything, but give her Arpège." Where America is concerned, radical Muslims believe, "Promise her anything, but give her jihad."

Like most religions, Islam for the most part forbids lying. According to the Quran, "Truly Allah guides not one who transgresses and lies" (Surah 40:28). However, when it comes to what happens in time of war, Islam actually encourages lying to the enemy.

In "Lying in Islam" Abdullah Al Araby writes:

> The Arabic word, "Takeyya", means "to prevent, " or guard against. The principle of Al Takeyya conveys the understanding that Muslims are permitted to lie as a preventive measure against anticipated harm to one's self or fellow Muslims. ...

> Unfortunately, when dealing with Muslims, one must keep in mind that Muslims can communicate something with apparent sincerity, when in reality they may have just the opposite agenda in their hearts. Bluntly stated, Islam permits Muslims to lie anytime that they perceive that their own well-being, or that of Islam, is threatened.

> In the sphere of international politics, the question is: Can Muslim countries be trusted to keep their end of the agreements that they sign with non-Muslim nations? It is a known Islamic practice, that when Muslims are weak they can agree with most anything. Once they become strong, then they negate what they formerly vowed.[38]

In his article, "The Lie is Different at Every Level," William P. Welty writes:

> A *Hudna* is a cease-fire. But when called within the context of *Al-Takeyya*, Islam's theology of military deception, it really amounts to a time-out to reload during a period of temporary weakness on the

part of the follower of Islam. In short, when Muslims are weak, they're admonished by the Qur'an and the *Hadith* to negotiate a peace treaty, or *Hudna*. When they're back on their military feet, so to speak, then they can break the treaty and go back to war ...

For five centuries—ever since militant Islam was defeated in Spain back in the '90s (the 1490s that is)—the West has enjoyed a relative time of quiet. And even though it lasted for 500 years, the lull in military activities still only amounts to a Hudna, a time of cease fire so that the Muslims could reload.

And reload they did. With WMDs.[39]

Westerners need to realize that the Islamist mindset sees all agreements with non-Muslim nations as being strictly temporary— until such time as Islam gets the upper hand again. Thus Dr. Ahmed Yousuf Abu Halabiya, member of the Palestinian Sharianic Rulings Council and Rector of Advanced Studies, Islamic University, was able to write: "We, the nation of Palestine, our fate from Allah is to be the vanguard in the war against the Jews until the resurrection of the dead, as the Prophet Muhammad said, 'The resurrection of the dead will not come until you do battle with the Jews and kill them.' We the Palestinians, are the vanguard in this issue, in this battle, whether we want to or whether we refuse. *All the agreements being made are temporary...* " [Emphasis added.][40]

## Radical Islamist Goals

While Islamists have many goals, they all spring from one ultimate objective: to establish a worldwide Islamic state, referred to as a Caliphate, ruled by an all-powerful head of state called a Caliph. This global theocracy would be governed by strict Shariah law. On the way towards establishing the Caliphate, present-day Islamists have a twofold agenda: they want to convert non-Muslim countries into Muslim countries, and they want to bring secular

Muslim countries under the control of Muslim religious law.

## Establishment of Theocratic Regimes in Muslim States

Not all Islamic violence is directed against non-Muslims. There is an old Arabic saying: "I and my brother against my cousin, I and my cousin against my neighbor, I and my neighbor against the world."[41] One of the goals of radical Islam is to establish Shariah, the Islamic law according to the Quran and Hadith, as the law of every land. Muslims believe that every country should be a Muslim country, and that every Muslim country should be a theocracy. Thus radical Muslims desire to bring about the rule of Muslim law in Muslim countries, even if it means overthrowing existing secular regimes already composed of Muslims. Militant Islam is just as militant towards secular Muslim states as it is towards Western countries.

## Independence for Muslim Minorities

While radical Islam has as its ultimate goal the establishment of global Muslim rule, an interim Islamist goal is the establishment of independent Muslim states for Muslim minorities who are living in non-Muslim countries. Pakistan, once a part of India, was created as an independent Muslim state. Now there is a separatist movement in the Indian State of Jammu & Kashmir seeking to carve yet another Muslim state out of India. This is similar to what the Muslims are working towards in Israel. Before Israel became a nation, the British divided Palestine into Transjordan and Palestine. Transjordan—originally a part of Palestine—eventually became Jordan, an Arab state. Even though they had already carved one Arab state out of Palestine, Britain then divided what remained of Palestine into Arab and Jewish territories. When Israel became a state, its territory comprised just a small part of what had once been the British Mandate of Palestine. And ever since 1967, Muslim Arabs have been trying to subdivide Israel yet again. But that's the subject of another chapter.

In addition to the Muslim separatist movements already mentioned, Muslim separatist movements also exist in Bosnia, Kosovo, Chechnya, Daghestan (former USSR), and Xinjiang Province (China).

## Suppression of Non-Muslim Ethnic and Cultural Minorities

Yet another radical Muslim goal is to suppress non-Muslim minorities who seek autonomy or independence within Muslim states. To Muslims, it may be all right for *Muslim* minorities to seek their independence, but the opposite does not hold true for *non-Muslim* ethnic and cultural minorities if they happen to live in a country where there are a lot of Muslims. Such suppression is behind the wars between the Islamic regime and the Christian minority in Southern Sudan, between the central Islamic government in Indonesia and the Christian inhabitants of East Timor, and the suppression of the Chinese and other ethnic minorities in Indonesia. I say "suppression," but often—as in Darfur, Sudan—this suppression is so severe that it qualifies as genocide.

Writing about the Sudanese conflict in FrontPageMagazine.com, Jamie Glazov asks, "Why is it that -- yet again -- another Arab League member is massacring its minority populations? Why is the Western media reluctant to identify the religion and ethnicity of the mass murderers and rapists?"[42]

Why, indeed? Mid-East expert Jon Lewis answered the question this way:

> The media in the United States is very uncomfortable in attributing religious motivations to violence. We see this in the case of the Palestinian suicide bombers who are often described as motivated by poverty and frustration, rather than by religious ideology. In Darfur, there is indeed a religious component to the violence; after all, the Khartoum government is an Islamo-fascist one.

What bothers me more about the media coverage of Darfur is its lack of historic context - Darfur is but one example of Arab racism toward non-Arabs within the broader "Arab world." The Darfur genocide, I believe, must be viewed not solely as a case of an Islamic jihad, but also as a case of Arab racism and should be seen as parallel to Saddam Hussein's genocide against Kurds and the Algerian government's repression of the Kabyles.

Remember: both the Kurds and Kabyles are primarily Sunni Muslims, at least in a nominal sense. I don't mean to downplay the Islamic jihad aspect; however, I think that we cannot understand the violence in Darfur (and Iraq, for that matter) without examining the persistence of intra-Muslim ethnic conflict in the region and Arab racism.[43]

## Once Muslim, Always Muslim

In his book *Future Jihad*, Walid Phares points out that "To Islamists, every land that was conquered—or technically, opened—during the *fatah* under a legitimate Islamic authority *cannot* revert back to the infidels."[44] This is especially true in the case of Israel, which must be seen as a special case. But it is also true of Spain, much of France, and parts of Russia and India. To the Islamic mind, if a nation was once an Islamic nation, it forever rightfully belongs to Islam and any current rule by infidels is seen as illegitimate. Thus another goal of radical Islam is to re-establish what they see as the "rightful" Muslim rule of formerly Muslim areas. Sooner or later, Westerners living in formerly Muslim territories can expect to be targeted by jihadists who firmly believe they have stolen that land from Islam.

## Establishment of New Muslim States throughout the World

Writing in *The Warriors of God*, A.S. Abraham and George Haddad summarize the Muslim goal of world domination this way:

To a considerable extent, all Muslims are fundamentalists, that is they believe that the *Qur'an*, the holy scripture of Islam is God's final complete and perfected revelation for all mankind. The *Qur'an* is therefore the supreme guide for the human race, the direct words of God, covering all aspects of human life transmitted directly to his last prophet and messenger, Muhammad.

Islam is God's plan for the world, every inch of it, not only just the Islamic regions. Islam is for everyone, whether one wants it or not. It is the duty of every Moslem to help expand the borders of Islam until every being on this planet acknowledges that "There is no God but Allah and Muhammad is his Messenger."[45]

Although world domination is the ultimate goal, as a short-term strategy radical Islam aims to neutralize the influence of foreign—particularly Western—civilizations situated on the fault lines with Islamic culture. Of course, radical Islam eventually plans to subdue the entire world. As a matter of priorities, however, it is the fault-line civilizations that are being targeted first—places where Muslim areas are adjacent to non-Muslim areas. As listed by Shaul Shay and Yoram Schweitzer[46], these fault-line conflicts and wars include:

- The Arab-Israeli conflict
- Conflicts between Sudan, Uganda, and Ethiopia (Christian).
- The war between Eritrea and Ethiopia (Christian).
- The conflict between Turkey and Greece, including Cyprus (Christian).
- The confrontation between Iraq and the USA and the West.
- The confrontation between Azerbaijan and Armenia (Christian).
- The confrontation between Afghanistan and Russia and its allies Tajikistan and Uzbekistan.

- The war between Pakistan and India (the Kashmir region).

## Muslim Jihadists Have Targeted You

As we have seen, radical Islam wants to convert the entire world, including you. Speaking as a Christian, I too would like to convert the world (to Christianity). The difference between me and radical Islam is that while I plan to do my part by preaching the Gospel, radical Islam is willing—and planning—to use warfare, terrorism, and weapons of mass destruction to achieve their goals. Islamic militancy has become a threat, not just to Israel, but to every non-Muslim nation. And if you are not a Muslim, Islamic militancy has become a threat to you.

*"We say to this West... By Allah, you will be defeated. You will be defeated in Palestine, and your defeat there has already begun. True, it is Israel that is being defeated there, but when Israel is defeated, its path is defeated, those who call to support it are defeated, and the cowards who hide behind it and support it are defeated. Israel will be defeated, and so will whoever supported or supports it. "*
Hamas chief Khaled Mashal, February 3, 2006[47]


# CHAPTER 4

# THE CURRENT WORLD WAR


William P. Welty asks, "How is it that only the Israelis know that World War III started on September 11, 2001?[48]

Like it or not, the War Against Terror is a World War. Like William P. Welty, some would call it World War III. Others (who also count the Cold War) would call it World War IV. Whatever its number, it is a global war.

Although has taken a long time for reality to sink in, by now many Americans do realize that we are in a war. Not only that, but we are in a war that was formally, if unilaterally, declared by one of the parties as early as February 1998. According to The 9/11 Commission report:

> In February 1998, the 40-year-old Saudi exile Usama Bin Ladin and a fugitive Egyptian physician, Ayman al Zawahiri, arranged from their Afghan headquarters for an Arabic newspaper in London to publish what they termed a fatwa issued in the name of a "World Islamic Front." A fatwa is normally an interpretation of Islamic law by a respected Islamic authority, but neither Bin Ladin, Zawahiri, nor the

three others who signed this statement were scholars of Islamic law. Claiming that America had declared war against God and his messenger, they called for the murder of any American, anywhere on earth, as the "individual duty for every Muslim who can do it in any country in which it is possible to do it."

Three months later, when interviewed in Afghanistan by ABC-TV, Bin Ladin enlarged on these themes. He claimed it was more important for Muslims to kill Americans than to kill other infidels. "It is far better for anyone to kill a single American soldier than to squander his efforts on other activities," he said. Asked whether he approved of terrorism and of attacks on civilians, he replied: "We believe that the worst thieves in the world today and the worst terrorists are the Americans. Nothing could stop you except perhaps retaliation in kind. We do not have to differentiate between military or civilian. As far as we are concerned, they are all targets." [49]

Although it came as a surprise on 9/11, in reality the Islamist war of terror has been developing for many years. It has its roots deep in Islamic culture, is embedded in the Islamic holy book, and—ever since the petrodollars began flowing in the middle of the twentieth century—it has been helped along by an endless flow of cash.

## The Roots of War

The United States emerged from the Cold War as the only true global power, never imagining that its power was about to be challenged on September 11, 2001—not by another actual nation, but by a terrorist organization that saw itself as the ideological heir of the Islamic empire, an empire founded by the prophet Muhammad that once stretched from the Atlantic to the Pacific— albeit not on the American subcontinents.

During the Cold War, and especially when it ended, a group of Muslims emerged who dreamed of restoring the Islamic empire so that it would once again stretch from the Atlantic to the Pacific, and once again be governed by Islamic law. This dream was especially attractive to Arabs who were disaffected and humiliated by poverty and defeat. Many feel that it was this very humiliation that led directly to the events of September 11, 2001. Flush with their success in Afghanistan after ousting the Soviet Union and angered by the presence of US troops on Islamic holy ground in Saudi Arabia, Osama bin Laden's terrorists longed to bring back the glory days of Islam. Some have said that Osama bin Laden dreamed of becoming the Caliph of a new caliphate—a global empire governed by Islamic law. Part of his game plan was to wage war on the United States.

At its height, the Islamic empire was one of the great civilizations in world history—economically, culturally, intellectually, and politically. However, at the end of World War I, Islamic civilization reached an all-time low when the Ottoman Empire collapsed. No longer could Muslims claim to have a multinational Islamic empire anywhere in the world. The vast non-Arab Muslim world—Pakistan (then part of India), Indonesia, Malaysia—had already been occupied by Europeans, but was again falling into chaos due to European decolonization. The collapse of the Ottoman Empire at the end of World War I combined with the disintegration of European imperialism to leave the Muslim world in a shambles.

The Arabs are a proud people. During much of the twentieth century, however, Arab pride suffered the decades of humiliation that was to become the breeding ground of the jihadist movement. Writing about this humiliation in an article in *The Guardian*, Egyptian journalist Hani Shukrallah says:

> How far back does one trace the sense of humiliation and deeply injured dignity at western hands that has been such a formative element of Arab awareness and self-image for decades? Do we

need to go as far back as the 1917 Balfour
Declaration, or as recently as the 1948 war, the
dispossession of the Palestinians and the resounding
and humiliating defeat of the combined armies of the
Arab world.

The 1948 war would be carved in common Arab
memory as Al-Nakba, the Catastrophe. And then
there was the Six-Day war, the resounding defeat of
Egypt, Syria and Jordan in June 1967 at Israel's
hand, resulting in the occupation of Sinai, the Golan
Heights and all that remained of the historic land of
Palestine. The sense of humiliation born out of June
1967 was perhaps the most shattering of all in
proportion to the immense hopes of emancipation
and restored national dignity that the wave of pan-
Arab nationalism, led and symbolised by Nasser's
leadership, had come to trigger. ... The humiliations
have been piled one on top of the other ever since.[50]

Many commentators, both Arab and Western, have pointed
towards an Arab sense of humiliation as being a root cause of
terrorist activity. In an article entitled "Arab intelligentsia walks a
tightrope," posted on Al-Jazeerah.info, Wissam S. Yafi says that
"After centuries of military defeat and humiliation by external
powers, some Arabs perceive their pride to be all that remains and
obstinately take counterintuitive positions and ones in apparent self-
disinterest - Palestinian suicide bombings of Israeli civilians *as
opposed to Israeli military targets* [emphasis added] being a case in
point."[51] (We would argue that *any* suicide bombings are a case in
point!)

Although suicide is condemned by Islamic law, Islamic
culture glorifies martyrs who give their lives in jihad. Rather than
going to hell like other suicides, these martyrs are believed to be
greatly rewarded in paradise: "Those who blow themselves up
almost daily in Israel and those who died on September 11 were
dying in the noblest of all causes, Jihad, which is an incumbent
religious duty, established in the Koran and in the Traditions as a

divine institution, and enjoined for the purpose of advancing Islam. While suicide is forbidden, martyrdom is everywhere praised, welcomed, and urged."[52]

In an *International Herald Tribune* article entitled "From Wounded Pride, a Deadly Rage Explodes," columnist Roger Cohen quotes retired Jordanian general Ali Shakri as saying that "The political system in the Arab world is broken. Nasserism, Baathism—all bankrupt. And religion has stepped in to fill the gap. What we have today is a culture of the humiliated." Cohen writes that some Islamic clerics have channeled that humiliation, "particularly among Palestinian and Arab youths, toward a cult of suicide bombings."[53]

In January 1979, the Shah of Iran was ousted by an Islamist revolution led by the Ayatollah Ruhollah Khomeini. This was a setback for the United States. Iran had been our ally and a stable source of oil, even during the Arab oil embargoes. Although many Americans mistakenly think of Iranians as being Arabs, Arabs and Iranians are ethnically different: the Iranians are descended from the Persians, while the Arabs are a Semitic people. However, most Iranians are Muslims despite their non-Arab origins. The Ayatollah took advantage of the unpopularity of the Shah's secular regime to create a populist theocratic republic based on Islamic culture and traditions and ruled by Islamic law. This was something that had never existed before, and the entire Islamic world was electrified.

Shortly thereafter—in November of that same year—the American Embassy in Teheran was seized, creating the Iranian hostage crisis that would last until the inauguration of Ronald Reagan and that would appear to the Islamic world to be a demonstration of American weakness. Meanwhile, the Cold War was still in progress. The Soviet Union was encircled by American and Allied troops. If the Soviets had been able break through to the Persian Gulf, taking control of the Saudi oil fields, the balance of power would have shifted dramatically, something the United States could not allow.

When the Soviets invaded Afghanistan and started building

airfields, Americans feared the worst: these airfields would put Soviet fighter aircraft within range of the Persian Gulf and the Strait of Hormuz. If the Soviets then chose to invade Iran, there would be very little America could do, short of dropping an atomic bomb. Because of this it was decided that the United States could not allow a Soviet victory in Afghanistan.

In order to keep the Soviets at bay, President Carter was persuaded to secretly sponsor a war of national liberation in Afghanistan, using the indigenous forces that were already resisting the Communist government there. One of the unintended consequences of this decision was to reach its fruition on September 11, 2001. Before the fall of the Soviet Union, radical Islamists saw the Soviet Union as Enemy Number One, mostly because it was an atheist state, but also because it had (as they saw it) usurped authority over a number of formerly Muslim lands. Muslims believe that once a land has been "opened" to Islam, it is rightfully Islam forevermore. The US, which was perceived by Muslims as a Christian nation, was also seen as an enemy of Islam; however the Soviets, because of their atheism, were seen as being worse.

Since US participation in the war in Afghanistan was to be covert, it had to be fought with covert funds. These funds were to come from Saudi Arabia. The Saudis badly needed a strong US, not only as a defense against the Soviets, but also against the Shiite regime in Iran. America needed Saudi funds and Saudi cultural and religious expertise. The religious expertise was necessary because Afghanistan's only unifying force was Islam. Afghanistan had very little nationalist feeling. It was a nation of tribes and clans, and its loyalty was to Islam.

Two important things took place at this time. The first was a matter of perception. The second was a matter of financing. In *America's Secret War*, George Friedman writes:

> . . . the US was doing much more than working with the Saudis. The US was relying on them, and the Saudis knew it. The perception grew among

Saudis that they were being called on to save the United States.

The Saudis chose not to finance this operation directly from government coffers. Rather, the Saudi government tapped into vast reservoirs of private resources, in order to maintain deniability and to help build consensus outside the government in Saudi Arabia for the adventure. Families like the wealthy bin Ladens turned over vast sums of money to help finance the mujahideen who were fighting the Soviets.[54]

After the fall of the Soviet Union, the Saudi perception that they were being called on to save the United States grew into the conviction that it was Islamist fighters who had saved the world from the Soviet threat. When the Soviet Union fell, America saw the war in Afghanistan as just one of several contributing factors. However, the Islamic world felt that the Soviet Union had been brought down by Islamic forces. After the victory, the private funding never went away, as wealthy Saudis continued to supply jihadists with the necessary finances. While the Americans considered the struggle over and done with, the jihadists simply turned their attention to their next big target. Unfortunately, that next big target was the United States.

In Afghanistan, the Saudi-US alliance had seemed to be a natural fit. The United States had already allied itself with Islamic monarchies like Iran (which by that time had already fallen) and Saudi Arabia. During the war in Afghanistan, Pakistan, too, became a US ally. At the time, Pakistan was fearful of being trapped between a Soviet-occupied Afghanistan and a pro-Soviet India. Internally, Pakistan was also torn between the secularism of its founders and the religious Islamism of much of its population.

In Afghanistan, the Saudis provided funding, personnel, and the recruitment of mujahideen to support the CIA's covert efforts to build a guerrilla movement in Afghanistan, while Pakistan provided training camps, logistics, bases of operations and the support of their intelligence service to provide the liaison with the Afghan resistance movement. Many of these resources would later be employed by anti-American jihadists. Thus the Afghan war created thousands of what have come to be known as "Afghan Alumni"—trained, battle-hardened Islamist warriors, armed and trained by the United States and also armed with captured Soviet weapons.

The war in Afghanistan was of overwhelming emotional and ideological importance to the Islamic world. It was the first time in centuries that an Islamic force had defeated a non-Islamic force—and the fact that the Soviet Union had been a superpower made the victory even sweeter. Moreover, the Soviet Union had been defeated, not just by Afghans, but by a multinational Islamist force, financed with Islamic money. While the United States saw itself as the driving force behind the Afghan resistance, the Muslim world gave the credit to Islamic warriors and Islamic money.

To make matters worse, after the war was over the United States did nothing to help the Islamist fighters who had been imported into Afghanistan to do their bidding. After the Soviet threat dissolved, America rapidly lost interest in Afghanistan. In his book *America's Secret War*, George Friedman gives us the following details:

> The United States, which had been instrumental in arming, training, and deploying these men, lost interest in Afghanistan once the Soviet Union withdrew its troops and began to collapse. Afghanistan was not of great strategic interest to the US, and the cost of maintaining its network of operatives—let alone its secret army—was high. The first Bush administration made a decision that was obvious at the time and disastrous in retrospect: to pull the plug on the Afghani operations. It shut down all operations and left its erstwhile allies dangling in the breeze.
>
> Many of these operatives had been functioning covertly in Afghanistan and Pakistan. Their own

passports and identity papers had been replaced by Afghan and Pakistani documents. That was standard operating procedure for everyone's protection. However, as the United States shut down its operations, it did not return the original papers—which were in Washington or had been destroyed—nor did it make any provisions for returning the Islamic international brigade to their homes. This was partly due to US indifference. Even more, however, it was a response to the pressure of allied Islamic governments, which didn't want these holy warriors back.[55]

Abandoned by the United States, betrayed by their own countries, the Afghan alumni now saw their own governments as collaborating with the Christians, Jews, and Hindus. What was needed, they felt, was a return to the Caliphate—a theocratic Islamic empire that would be ruled by Islamic law. Obviously, such an empire wouldn't come into being overnight. What was needed, they felt, was one test case that would serve as an example to the rest of the Islamic world:

> The country that could most readily serve as the springboard to the Caliphate was Afghanistan. If a government of the faithful could be established in Afghanistan, then it could serve as both the core and the base of operations. For "the base"—or "Al Qaeda" in Arabic—to be established, a movement of the faithful, built around pious students—or Taliban—had to be created. The religious students could run Afghanistan, and within Afghanistan, the base could be established. In other words, the Taliban would govern Afghanistan while Al Qaeda was established to wage a war in the rest of the world.[56]

While Osama bin Laden and Al Qaeda were quietly gaining strength, other events were taking place in the Middle East that would also be understood differently by Muslims and Americans. When George Bush, Sr. decided to send troops to Saudi Arabia because of Saddam Hussein's invasion of Kuwait, Bush anticipated gratitude from the Arab nations. After all, America was saving an Islamic state, Kuwait, from being obliterated. Once again, the American perception was radically different from the Islamic point of view.

The Saudi government had their own reasons for allowing America to base troops in Saudi Arabia during Desert Shield and Desert Storm. However, this decision was highly unpopular with Saudi religious fundamentalists.

> To the Wahabi religious in the Kingdom, the decision was outrageous. The Arabian Peninsula was the birthplace of Islam, where Muhammad launched the campaign that created the Islamic empire. It is the home of Mecca and Medina, the holy cities of Islam. The presence of Christian troops on this soil—at the invitation of the Royal Family, no less, was a fundamental violation of the law. Moreover, regardless of Saddam's foul nature, allowing Christians to invade Muslim lands from Saudi Arabia was unacceptable.[57]

At this point in time, Islamic fundamentalists—who had been united against the communists—were divided on how best to deal with America.

Saudi Arabian policy had always been a long-term one of making inroads from the inside, acquiring influence in Washington and the business and academic communities. Its jihad, if you will, has been one of propaganda, publicity and politics, using petrodollars to spread the cause of Islam. Not just in the United States, but also around the world, the royal family of Saudi Arabia has chosen to spread its ideology through massive government funding of religious and sociocultural institutions.

Saudi Arabians outside the royal family wanted faster

results—and they also strenuously objected to allowing American troops to enter Saudi Arabia. Osama bin Laden, in particular, was aghast at the idea of allowing US forces to pollute the Muslims' holy land.

> In audiences with the monarchy's top leaders, Osama bin Laden pleaded with them to organize the Islamic resistance against the Baathist occupation of Kuwait. He begged them not to allow the infidels to deploy on Muslim lands, especially in Arabia, the land of the Prophet, which had been purged of Jews and Christians thirteen centuries ago. He asked the regime to authorize him to lead the Islamist jihad against the Baathists. In reality, he wanted to kill two birds with one stone. By pounding Saddam's forces in Kuwait and possibly inside Iraq, he wanted to return as a leader in the Wahabi country. His real strategic aim was to be received as a commander of the jihadists and eventually, in a historic fantasy, as a newly anointed caliph. . . . His dreams shattered when his own Wahabi rulers dismissed his plans, ignored his jihadist achievements in Afghanistan, and in the worst insult of all, extended their invitation to the very archenemies he wanted to fight next: the infidel Americans.[58]

## Signs of Weakness

One of the reasons Al Qaeda felt it could attack America with relative impunity was the way in which the US had failed to respond to previous attacks with the severity they deserved. In fact, our lack of response to the bombing of the US Marine barracks in 1983 has actually been cited by Osama bin Laden as one of the reasons he felt he could attack the US with impunity:

> According to former Navy secretary John F. Lehman, Osama bin Laden has "directly credited the Marine bombing" and the lack of US retaliation as

encouraging his jihadi movement to believe they could attack the United States with impunity.

"The first shots in the war on terror we are in now were fired in Beirut in October 1983," says [Marine Col. Tim] Geraghty. "The [Bush] administration is now doing exactly what we need to be doing, attacking the enemies of freedom where they live instead of letting them attack us in our home."

But the failure to strike back against Iran and Syria in 1983 was a dreadful mistake, he says.

"This was an act of war. We knew who the players were. And, because we didn't respond, we emboldened these people to increase the violence."[59]

As I have said before, Osama bin Laden attacked on 9/11 because he felt he could. Additionally, the attack on 9/11 was meant to rally the troops to the cause of Islam. Testifying before the National Commission on Terrorist Attacks upon the United States, Rohan Gunaratna said: "The defeat of the 'communist army' by the ideology of Islamism (and material support from the West and the Middle East) reinforced the belief that the United States, the remaining superpower too could be defeated through guerrilla warfare and terrorism. As the proclaimed vanguard of the struggle, Al Qaeda attacked America's most outstanding economic, military and political landmarks on September 11, 2001, to show the way to the Islamic movements, that the US too could be attacked and destroyed."[60]

As we said in the beginning of this chapter, we are in a world war. The United States is under attack, and we are under attack by an enemy who will attack us again at any sign of weakness on our part. This is not a time for rhetoric and posturing, for the sort of thing I like to call dancing with Islam's assassins. This is a time when acts of war must be dealt with by military means. The Bible teaches that there *is* a time for war: "A time to love, and a time to hate; a time of war, and a time of peace"

(Ecclesiastes 3:8).

    As any jihadist would be able to tell you, this is a time of war.

# CHAPTER 5

# AN AMERICAN HIROSHIMA

The next American "9/11" could be a nuclear bomb.

In his article, "Pakistan & Dangers of Nuclear Jihad," B. Raman of the South Asia Analysis Group points out that "Pakistan is the original birth place of the concept of the nuclear jihad, which highlighted the need for an Islamic atomic bomb and advocated the right and the religious obligation of the Muslims to acquire weapons of mass destruction (WMD) and use them, if necessary, to protect their religion. The jihadi terrorists and their ideologues in Pakistan perceived the nuclear weapon as the ultimate weapon of retribution against States which they viewed as enemies of Islam, particularly the USA and Israel."[61]

Raman explains that "What is new about jihadi terrorism is the gravitation of a number of students of science or working scientists to the jihadi organizations to help the terrorists in their jihad. While the students of science came to the jihadi organizations from many Islamic countries of the world, working scientists came mainly from Pakistan."[62] He goes on to say that "Pakistan has been the epicentre of State-sponsored nuclear proliferation since the late 1980s. Having benefited from funds contributed by Libya, Iran and

Saudi Arabia for its clandestine military nuclear project, the Pakistan State had to agree to requests from these countries for helping them in acquiring a similar capability."[63]

Whatever their motives, we now know that Pakistan has also cooperated with North Korea's missile program. We also know that Pakistan has been complicit in the transfer of nuclear technologies to Iran and Libya. Raman points out that "Even if one were to accept [Pakistani President] Musharraf's unconvincing arguments that this was a rogue operation by greedy scientists without the knowledge of the military, these concerns would only be aggravated and not lessened because if greedy scientists were prepared to help other States in return for money, they would be equally capable of selling material and expertise to jihadi terrorist organizations such as Al Qaeda, which can pay as well as these Islamic States."[64]

While Americans certainly have cause to be concerned about nuclear proliferation from one Islamic state to another, we have even more reason to worry about terrorist organizations like Al Qaeda, which answer to nobody but themselves and which do not concern themselves with traditional international diplomacy.

Writing in the August 11, 2004 edition of *The New York Times*, Nicholas D. Kristoff said that reports had regularly surfaced in the intelligence community that Al Qaeda had obtained a nuclear weapon from the Former Soviet Union. At that time, those reports had not yet been confirmed, but Kristoff said, "We do know several troubling things: Al Qaeda negotiated for the $1.5 million purchase of uranium (apparently of South African origin) from a retired Sudanese cabinet minister; its envoys traveled repeatedly to Central Asia to buy weapons-grade nuclear materials; and Osama bin Laden's top deputy, Ayman al-Zawahiri, boasted, 'We sent our people to Moscow, to Tashkent, to other Central Asian states, and they negotiated, and we purchased some suitcase [nuclear] bombs.'"[65]

According to the July 12, 2005 G2Bulletin, "At least two fully assembled and operational nuclear weapons are believed to be hidden in the United States already, according to G2B intelligence sources and an upcoming book, 'The al-Qaida Connection: International Terrorism, Organized Crime and the Coming Apocalypse,' by former FBI consultant Paul L. Williams. The cities chosen as optimal targets are New York, Miami, Los Angeles, Philadelphia, Chicago, San Francisco, Las Vegas, Boston and Washington, D.C." These are the nine US cities with the highest Jewish populations."[66]

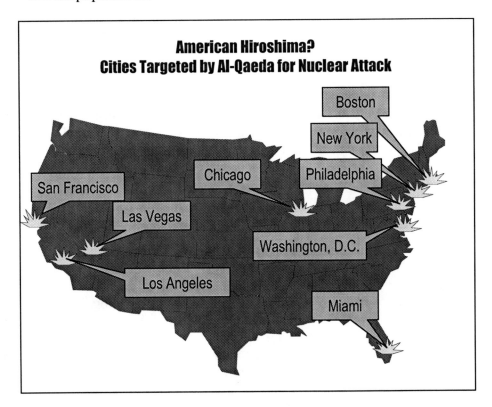

**American Hiroshima?**
**Cities Targeted by Al-Qaeda for Nuclear Attack**

In April 2006, the G2 Bulletin reported:

MI6, Britain's secret intelligence service, has identified six Pakistani scientists working in Iran's nuclear bomb program who have been "advising al-

Qaida on how to weaponize fissionable materials it
has now obtained."

MI6 and the International Atomic Energy
Agency believe the scientists have played a major
role in enabling Iran to be "well advanced in
providing uranium enriched materials for nuclear
bombs," said Alexander Cirilovic, a nuclear
terrorism expert in Paris.

Both high-level MI6 and CIA sources have
confirmed the scientists would only have been
allowed to assist al-Qaida with the authority of
Iran's unpredictable President Mahmoud
Ahmadinejad.[67]

The same article quotes Alexander Cirilovic, a nuclear
terrorism expert in Paris, as saying that "Depending on the quality
of the fissionable material bin Laden has obtained, the combined
scientific skills would be able to create considerably more than a
'dirty bomb.'"

Michael Scheuer, who once headed the CIA's Osama bin
Laden desk and is now a special advisor to the bin Laden unit, says
that an al-Qaida nuclear attack is almost inevitable:

About the prospects of a nuclear terrorist strike
on the US by al-Qaida, he says: "I don't believe in
inevitability. But I think it's pretty close to being
inevitable. ... Yes, I think it's probably a near thing."

Scheuer points out that bin Laden has
announced his intentions.

"He secured from a Saudi sheik named Hamid
bin Fahd a rather long treatise on the possibility of
using nuclear weapons against the Americans," he
said. "Specifically, nuclear weapons. And the
treatise found that he was perfectly within his rights
to use them. Muslims argue that the United States is
responsible for millions of dead Muslims around the
world, so reciprocity would mean you could kill
millions of Americans."[68]

Hamid Mir, bureau Chief of Islamabad for Geo TV and author of a forthcoming biography of Osama bin Laden, has interviewed countless members of al-Qaida and the Taliban. In a recent interview, with *World Threats'* Ryan Mauro, he said:

> At least two Al-Qaeda operatives claimed that the organization smuggled suitcase nukes inside America. But I have no details on who did it. But I do have details about who smuggled uranium inside America and how.
>
> I am very careful when speaking about Al-Qaeda's nuclear capabilities. I've met many people in Al-Qaeda who have claimed that uranium and nuclear bombs were smuggled to America, and I'll quote them in my book. However, when I speak for myself, I don't rely on claims by Al-Qaeda. I rely upon my own investigations.[69]

## Electromagnetic Pulse (EMP) Attacks

When they think of nuclear weapons, most people think about things like radiation and fallout. An electromagnetic pulse attack, however, would leave most people unharmed while creating havoc in our infrastructure.

According to the Department of Homeland Security, "A nuclear weapon detonated in or above the earth's atmosphere can create an electromagnetic pulse (EMP), a high-density electrical field. EMP acts like a stroke of lightning but is stronger, faster and briefer. EMP can seriously damage electronic devices connected to power sources or antennas. This includes communication systems, computers, electrical appliances, and automobile or aircraft ignition systems. The damage could range from a minor interruption to actual burnout of components. Most electronic equipment within 1,000 miles of a high-altitude nuclear detonation could be affected. Battery powered radios with short antennas generally would not be affected. Although EMP is unlikely to harm most people, it could harm those with pacemakers or other implanted electronic devices."[70]

An EMP attack doesn't sound all that bad until you consider its ramifications. In a March 2005 press release entitled "One Way We Could Lose the War on Terror," quoted below in its entirety, US Senator Jon Kyle spells out what could happen and warns this country that we must do what we can to be prepared:

> Last week the Senate Judiciary Committee's Subcommittee on Terrorism, Technology and Homeland Security, which I chair, held a hearing on a major threat to the United States, not only from terrorists but from rogue nations like North Korea.
>
> An electromagnetic pulse (EMP) attack over American soil, one of the expert witnesses at the hearing said, is one of only a few ways that America could be essentially defeated by our enemies, terrorist or otherwise. A single nuclear weapon, detonated at the right altitude, would produce an electromagnetic pulse that - depending on its location and size - would knock out power grids and other electrical systems across much of the country, for months if not years.
>
> Few if any people would die right away. But the long-term loss of electricity would essentially bring our society to a halt. Communication would be almost impossible. Powerless refrigerators would leave food rotting in warehouses, marooned by a lack of transportation as those vehicles still operable simply run out of gas (which can't be pumped without electricity). The unavailability of clean water would quickly threaten public health, not to mention leave the inevitable fires raging unchecked. As we have seen in areas of natural and other disasters, this kind of scenario often results in a fairly rapid breakdown of social order.
>
> Our society has grown so dependent on computer and other electrical systems that we have created our own Achilles' heel of vulnerability,

ironically much more so than less developed nations. Deprived of power in occasional blackouts, we are in many ways helpless. Typically, power is restored relatively quickly, but a large-scale burnout caused by broad EMP attack would create a much more difficult situation. Not only would there be nobody nearby to help, it could take years to replace destroyed equipment. Transformers for regional substations, for example, are huge and are no longer manufactured in the United States.

Essentially those in the affected area would find themselves transported back to the United States of the 1880s, for months if not years - a threat that might sound straight out of Hollywood, but is very real. FBI Director Robert Mueller has confirmed new intelligence that suggests Al Qaeda is trying to acquire and use weapons of mass destruction. Iran has surprised intelligence analysts by describing the mid-flight explosions of missiles fired from ships on the Caspian Sea as "successful" tests. North Korea exports missile technology around the world; SCUDs can easily be purchased on the open market for about $100,000 apiece. And Russia's rusting nuclear arsenal is highly vulnerable.

The attraction of an EMP attack to a terrorist organization is in its simplicity. Hitting a particular target, like a city, is difficult with a SCUD. But it is relatively simple to simply launch one, off a seagoing freighter for example, and detonate it at the right altitude.

Fortunately, preparing key infrastructure systems and stockpiling backup equipment like transformers is both feasible and relatively inexpensive, according to a comprehensive report on the EMP threat by a commission of prominent experts. But it will take leadership by the Department of Homeland Security, the Defense Department, and other federal agencies, along with support from Congress, all of which has yet to materialize.

The landmark 9/11 Commission report stated that our biggest failure was one of "imagination." No one imagined that terrorists would do what they did on September 11. Today few can conceive of the possibility that terrorists could bring American society to its knees by knocking out our power supply from several miles in the atmosphere. But this time we've been warned, and we'd better be prepared to respond.[71]

During the Cold War, an EMP attack would have been seen as the first step in a nuclear attack. Today, while both China and Russia would be able to launch major nuclear strikes against the US, we also need to worry about nuclear rogue states and non-state actors that are unable to fight a full-scale nuclear war. According to Jack Spencer of the Heritage Foundation:

> The emergence of nuclear rogue states results in a completely new strategic calculation. Since no rogue nation has the capacity to fight a general nuclear war, an EMP blast would not be a precursor of full-scale nuclear war. Furthermore, since an EMP blast is unlikely to kill anyone directly or to be followed by a nuclear strike that would annihilate U.S. cities, the United States is less likely to retaliate and destroy an entire nation of innocent people as punishment for the decisions of a rogue leader. It is simply unclear how the U.S. would respond to such an attack.
>
> The difficulty of developing a clear response to EMP is due primarily to the unique nature of the threat. It is unclear, for example, what would constitute a "proportional response" to an explosion that takes place in space without being seen or heard, yet instantaneously devastates society or a military force while resulting in no initial loss of life or

physical destruction. Furthermore, there is a dearth of academic or legal analysis by which to guide such policies because, until very recently, few took the threat seriously. This is especially so in the context of rogue states or transnational groups.

The simple motivation for a rogue state to use its limited nuclear arsenal in an EMP strike against the United States is that an EMP attack maximizes the impact of a few warheads while minimizing the risk of retaliation. This profound decrease in risk for rogue leaders could impel them to use EMP to offset overwhelming U.S. conventional power on the battlefield. While EMP may not precede general nuclear war, it could be used as an opening salvo in a conventional war. Nations with small numbers of nuclear missiles, such as North Korea or Iran, may consider an EMP attack against U.S. forces in a region, to degrade the U.S. military's technological advantage, or against the United States' national electronic infrastructure.[72]

In my opinion, the US response to an EMP attack would greatly depend on the political party that happened to be in power. Those of us who are Christians really need to pray that God will put the right people in place during our next presidential election, and that He will give President Bush and our next President the wisdom they need to respond in any crisis.

*"The determination of the Kingdom to support Islam and Islamic institutions to the best of its ability was evident from the formation of the Kingdom by King Abdul Aziz but it was only when oil revenues began to generate real wealth that the Kingdom could fulfill its ambitions of spreading the word of Islam to every corner of the world ..."*
Saudi government weekly Ain-Al-Yaqeen[73]

# CHAPTER 6

# MUSLIM PROPAGANDA

On February 3, 2006, speaking from a Damascus mosque, Hamas chief Khaled Mashal said, "Tomorrow, our nation will sit on the throne of the world. This is not a figment of the imagination, but a fact." As reported in Jerusalem Newswire, "Mashal went on to point out the obvious reason why the West continues inching itself closer to defeat by pandering to what it believes are the "moderate" Muslim masses: 'They do not understand the Arab or Muslim mentality, which rejects the foreigner.'"[74]

In June 2007, shortly before this revised edition went to press, Hamas took control of the Gaza strip. In their ministry newsletter, Reuven and Mary Doron pointed out that "For all practical purposes, Israel now has to deal with another Islamic terror state on its southern border, located only 45 miles from the main population centers of the Tel Aviv Metro area where nearly 2.5 million Israelis reside."[75] The Dorons summed up the Gaza situation as follows:

> In August 2005 Israel evacuated the Gaza Strip (which is known as the Disengagement), dismantled its prosperous agricultural communities, while every Jewish family was forced to leave their homes.

These communities were considered the most beautiful in all of Israel, having turned barren desert into fertile fields with green houses that produced beautiful flowers and remarkable vegetables, with exports to Europe alone amounting to over 100 million US dollars per year.

Pulling out of Gaza and leaving behind this rich infrastructure as an economic backbone enabling the Palestinians to rule their own lives turned into a disaster. Instead of prospering in its self determination, Gaza has turned into a living hell. Not only have thousands of rockets been fired from Gaza into Israeli southern civilian communities since the Disengagement, but violence and anarchy have destroyed the lives of the Palestinians themselves. Rather than taking over the fruitful Israeli farms, they have looted and destroyed them, transforming the grounds into terrorist training camps and rocket ramps.

Six months following Israel's withdrawal from Gaza, the Palestinians elected terror organization Hamas into power, and a make-shift Palestinian government was formed between (radical) Hamas and (semi-moderate) Fatah. It didn't last long. Rather than developing economic opportunities for the desperate Palestinian population, their leaders vowed to destroy Israel, disqualified themselves from International aid, and have spent dirty Iranian money to build up their military and terror capabilities. Today, these weapons are destroying their own people.

Since Hamas came into power, thousands of Palestinian Arabs have been killed and wounded in internal fighting. According to Palestinian statistics, more than 200,000 Palestinians have fled Gaza to seek shelter in other nations, and 45 000 of them are presently applying for visas to leave in spite of a Hamas ruling against leaving. The International community's response is, as always, to throw more money at the problem. But these funds, as in the past, will only make the corrupt mafia Palestinian leadership richer, and fund their terror machinery.

Some Palestinian civilians in Gaza told the media in recent days that they are fed up with their own governing bodies and that "we should be so lucky as to see the return of the Israeli occupation." Yet, despite the horrific bloodbath within Gaza, Kassam rockets continue to be launched against civilian Israeli communities....The truth is that the Palestinian people are not a national entity and will never become one. If their sad history during the last 100 years proves anything at all, it proves the fact that they are unable to self-govern and shouldn't be expected to do so. *Their existence as a distinct people group with artificially constructed national aspirations is a political trick meant to undermine and weaken Israel's position and claim in and to the Promised Land* [emphasis added]. No amount of lies or denial can change this truth.[76]

One reason the West does not understand the Muslim mentality is that there has been a concerted public relations effort to lull Westerners into believing that Islam is a peace-loving religion. Untold millions of petrodollars have been spent, especially by Saudi Arabia, on propaganda directly aimed at influencing the opinions of both Muslims and Westerners. These messages are not the same. Muslims are indoctrinated with a fundamentalist "party line" that glorifies jihad; Westerners, on the other hand, are told how moderate and peace loving "true Muslims" are.

Speaking of the propaganda that targets Muslims, Mamoun Fandy said:

Although we are winning the war against the organization called al-Qaeda, we seem to be losing the cultural war. This means that in the Arab and the Muslim World, al-Qaeda and its affiliate organizations continue to draw on a new pool of recruits. The Arab and the Muslim media is the nebulous area where secret relations amongst states and terrorist organizations are forged. This culture of terrorism in not a sentiment; it is an industry. Their people and governments who finance these newspapers and TV stations that promote al-Qaeda and its ideas. Many leaders of states and industries in the Arab and the Muslim world - even America's friends - have failed to take a clear stand in terms of their relationship with al-Qaeda and the extremist ideas they promote and the money these states spend of their TV and newspapers. In many Arab newspapers and TV programs, Ben Laden can appear as a hero- and even if al-Qaeda is not named, its ideas and "victory" over America are implicitly applauded. This peaks in Qatar's al-Jazeera and the Lebanese channels and El-Osboa newspaper in Cairo which recently praised "any one who put a bullet in the heart of any American." [77]

While Islamist propaganda aimed at Muslims glorifies acts of terror and suicide, disinformation aimed at the West from the very same sources does its best to whitewash the culture of terrorism, making it appear the work of a minority of fanatics who don't really represent Islam as a whole. Dr. Walid Phares, who was born and raised in Lebanon but relocated to the United States in 1990, [78] says that "We in the West have been at the mercy of those who where [sic] supposed to translate and explain an entire ideology but instead sanitized it and camouflaged it."[79]

Summarizing a portion of Phares' book, *Future Jihad*, reporter Rosemary McDonough writes:

Though Islamists (specifically, Wahabi Muslims) are stuck in the past, they aren't stupid. They know that, despite their success on 9/11, they can not possibly defeat the greatest infidel, America, militarily - at least not without nuclear weapons. So until they get them, their plan is to observe and infiltrate Western society, slowly and patiently, and hoist the West by its own petard.

How? Phares describes a "Wahabi Circle" that works like this. First, the largely Saudi Wahabi lobby comes to America and makes friends in our oil-dependent, diversity-embracing society. Then they pass out money - to lobbying groups and elite universities. Next, the leading universities, through Wahabi-influenced curriculum and faculty, produce the academic experts and policy analysts that America relies on for foreign affairs. These "experts" influence the media - which in turn influences public opinion - which then influences the government - which becomes even more susceptible to Wahabi influence - and the cycle continues. Phares calls this process "the blurring of American vision" - where all evidence of infiltration is before us, but no one sees it.[80]

Financially, the biggest player in propagandizing the West is the kingdom of Saudi Arabia. Testifying before the United States Senate Judiciary Committee, Steven Emerson, the Executive Director of The Investigative Project on Terrorism, had this to say:

In the years prior to 9-11, the US government paid little attention to the flow of money and religious propaganda exported worldwide from Saudi Arabia. During that period, an elaborate network of Saudi-funded and directed charities, foundations and Islamic propagation centers were created, which in turn funded Islamic organizations, schools and radical movements around the world. Because of its vast petrodollar riches, Saudi Arabia's version of Islam -- a puritanical interpretation often described in short hand as Wahabism -- succeeded in indoctrinating young Muslims, controlling the religious direction of major Islamic religious institutions and in extending the Wahabist doctrine to the four corners of the Earth. The paper trail of Saudi money, funneled through a vast network of charities and religious organizations, has led to some of the most violent terrorist groups in the world, including Al-Qaeda and Hamas.

Saudi officials have long asserted publicly and in private discussions with US officials that the government cannot be held responsible for the actions of non-governmental groups, private donors and corporations, the media and religious leaders. But in fact, much of the non-governmental network in Saudi Arabia was created by Saudi government officials to provide an arm's length relationship and has long been funded by Saudi government line items or by members of the Royal Family. The Wahabist-dominated religious hierarchy in Saudi Arabia was and is tightly controlled by the Saudi regime and Royal Family.

According to the official website of King Fahd bin Abdul Aziz, "It is difficult to find a corner of the world where Saudi Arabia, under King Fahd, has not made a contribution, either in humanitarian aid (which flows forth as soon as a need is recognized) or in promulgating Islam by building Mosques and Islamic centers and by distributing copies of the Holy Quran"[81]

In January 2005, the Center for Religious Freedom released an 89-page report entitled "Saudi Publications on Hate Ideology Fill American Mosques." According to their news release, the report was based on "a year-long study of over two hundred original documents, all disseminated, published or otherwise generated by the government of Saudi Arabia and collected from more than a dozen mosques in the United States."[82] The report itself can be downloaded from http://freedomhouse.org/religion/.

According to this report, "... not all the books in such mosques espouse extremism and not all extremist works are Saudi. Saudi Arabia, however, is overwhelmingly the state most responsible for the publications on the ideology of hate in America."[83]

Former Secretary of State George P. Shultz, clearly had Saudi Arabia in mind when he said:

> Some states have made tacit deals with foreign terrorists, allowing them offices in their cities in return for a pledge of immunity. Some states have tolerated, subsidized, and facilitated homegrown terrorist groups with the understanding that those groups will not attempt to overthrow national leaders, creating a kind of grotesque protection racket. Some states pump out huge volumes of propaganda against other states in an effort to direct terrorists within their borders toward external targets. Some states, in a desperate search for legitimacy, have invited religions that foster terrorists to take over substantial sectors of governmental activity on condition that some functions, such as foreign affairs and defense policy, will be left alone. And some states secretly, but undeniably, support terrorism directly as a matter of state policy.[84]

In a symposium entitled, "Saudi Arabia: Friend or Foe," Jamie Glazov of Front Page Magazine interviewed Daniel Pipes, Director of the Middle East Forum and the author of *Militant Islam Reaches America*. He asked Pipes, "Do you think American policymakers have dealt competently with the KSA (Kingdom of Saudi Arabia)? Pipes replied, "No, I can think of no country where American interests are less well upheld than with Saudi Arabia. The Saudi ambassador to Washington in part once explained why: 'If the reputation . . . builds that the Saudis take care of friends when they leave office,' Bandar bin Sultan said, 'you'd be surprised how much better friends you have who are just coming into office.' In part, the lack of assertiveness results from the phenomenon so well described by a former US ambassador to Riyadh: 'it's amusing to see how some Americans liquefy in front of a foreign potentate, just because he's called a prince.'"[85]

Why is Islam winning the propaganda war in America? Could it simply be because Saudi Arabian petrodollars have bought and paid for all too many academics, politicians, leaders of multinational corporations, and even journalists?

In Princes of Darkness, Laurent Murawiec says: "University chairs in the West have been very richly endowed by King Fahd. As one of the most astute observers, the former English diplomat, John Kelly, explains, "the rulers of the Arab oil states are neither simple philanthropists nor disinterested patrons.... They expect a return upon their donations to institutions of learning and their subsidies to publishing houses; whether it be in the form of subtle propaganda on behalf of Arab or Islamic causes, or the preferential admission of their nationals, however unqualified ... Or the publication of the kind of sycophantic flim-flam about themselves and their countries which now clutters sections of the Western press and even respectable periodical literature."[86]

Make no mistake about it: Arab-funded propaganda is a definite part of jihad.

# CHAPTER 7

# SUICIDE BOMBERS

Chinese general and author Sun Tzu is reported to have said, "Know your enemy and know yourself and you can fight a hundred battles without disaster."

Every weapon of mass destruction needs a delivery system. Sometimes that delivery system is conventional, as when a nuclear bomb is part of a missile system. Terrorists, however, seem to favor human beings as an integral part of their delivery systems. This gives rise to suicide attacks—attacks in which the attacker(s) plan to die for the cause.

The low cost, high visibility and high lethality of such suicide attacks have made them a favorite with terrorist groups. As of this writing, the September 11, 2001 suicide attacks using hijacked airplanes were the largest and most destructive on record, but who knows what further terrors jihadists might have up their sleeves?

Westerners associate suicide attacks with modern times: the Japanese kamikaze pilots of World War II and the militant Islamists of today. But suicide attacks have existed throughout history: Bible students will recall Samson's suicide attack on a Philistine temple: "And Samson said, 'Let me die with the Philistines!' And he bowed himself with all his might; and the house fell upon the lords, and upon all the people that were therein. So the dead which he slew at his death were more than they which he slew in his life" (Judges 16:30).

In modern times, most suicide attacks have been carried out using vehicles and/or explosive materials, which is why we so often speak of a "suicide bomber." If a suicide attack goes as planned, the attacker is killed upon impact and/or detonation—in addition to killing and/or injuring many innocent people. What sort of person would do such a thing—kill not only himself but others who have never done a thing to harm him?

## A Suicide Bomber's Profile

Islamist suicide bombers are generally not the crazed, unstable people Westerners would at first assume them to be. Most suicide bombers are not mentally ill. The leaders of the groups that organize the attacks invest a lot of time and money in preparation for them: they want to entrust them to reliable recruits who can carry out their missions, not to mentally unstable people. Many suicide bombers are educated and come from middle class homes. They see their cause as righteous and worthwhile and believe that they will be rewarded for their sacrifice in the afterlife. Islamist suicide bombers are not always men: in recent years there have been more and more reports of suicide bombers who were women and children. Islamist suicide bombers need not necessarily be Arabs: it is reported that Islam is the fastest-growing religion in America today.

Finally, "suicide" bombers are not always truly *suicide* bombers: there have been reports of some "suicide" bombers being chained or tied to vehicles' steering wheels, or where the bomb in a vehicle was remotely detonated. Even more disturbing, there has been at least one instance where a developmentally disabled child was used in an attack:

Terrorists used a disabled child as a suicide bomber on election day, Iraqi interior minister Falah al-Naqib said today.

In all, 44 people were killed in a total of 38 bomb attacks on polling stations. Police at the scene of one the Baghdad blasts said the bomber appeared to have Down's syndrome.[87]

So what is your Islamic suicide terrorist like? He or she may be a man, a woman, or a child. He/she most probably of sound mind, with the backing of a terrorist organization behind him. He/she most likely believes his/her cause is just and wishes to die for that cause, although there is a chance that he/she has been duped. He/she may have Down's syndrome. You cannot tell him/her by looking. He/she may not have known a bomb was in the car.

# CHAPTER 8

# THE GEOGRAPHY OF TERRORISM

The War on Terror is not conventional warfare, in that specific nations are not necessarily the root of the problem. In his statement to the National Commission on Terrorist Attacks Upon the United States, Mamoun Fandy made this abundantly clear. He said:

> Terrorism in the Muslim world can be drawn as a triangle between three points: states that harbor the terrorists, the terrorists themselves; and finally the Islamic movements that provide the pool of recruits and the intellectual drive and justification for acts of terrorism. Our current policy addresses two elements of this triangle, terrorist organizations and states that harbor terrorists. We have failed however to adequately understand the nature of the third component of the triangle of terror and its importance. That third component is the role played by broad anti-American movements such as the Muslim Brotherhood in making terrorism appear legitimate in the eyes of ordinary Arabs and

Muslims. In fact, movements are becoming more powerful than states. One can only look at Lebanon to see who wields more power, the Lebanese state or the radical Hibzbullah [*sic*]? After driving Israel out of southern Lebanon, Hizbullah gained more influence in Lebanese politics. Many Arab leaders went to Lebanon to congratulate them for liberating southern Lebenon [*sic*]. These leaders did not visit with Hareiri, the prime minister, instead they visited with sheikh Nasralla, the leader of Hizbullah. The Lebanese model boosted the role of movements in Arab society over the role of the state. This is why I say that movements matter most. This should come before states as we consider the significant pieces in phase two of the war on terrorism.[88]

As Islam becomes more and more militant, it becomes more and more important for Westerners to know who the players are. We need to know which countries are mainly Muslim—and what kinds of Muslims live in those countries. (For a very basic listing of Muslim countries, see "Countries with a Large Muslim Population," on page 89. However, as Mamoun Fandy pointed out, we aren't just dealing with countries; we are also dealing with terrorist organizations.)

As the nightly news has taught us, in many cases it is important to know, not just that a country has a Muslim majority, but what *kind* of Muslim is prevalent in that particular country. In *Journey of the Jihadist*, Fawaz A. Gerges writes:

> There are many kinds of Islamists—from moderate to mainstream to militant. There are different forms of Islamism, just as there are many forms of Islam—Sunni, Shiite, Salafi, Sufi, and Wahabi being the major ones—all of which reflect different tribal (and now national) distinctions and philosophical traditions (such as which religious texts should receive greater or lesser emphasis). Palestinian Islamists are generally Sunni; Egyptian,

Sunni; Saudi, a blend of Salafi and Wahhabi; Iranian, Shiite. These overlap, interact, and intersect in ways that affect alliances and perspectives. Some are more intolerant than others. They all share the goal of establishing Islamic governments based on shariah, Qur'anic law. Beyond that, few see eye to eye ...[89]

*The 9/11 Commission Report* explains the different streams of Islam this way:

Islam is divided into two main branches, Sunni and Shia. Soon after the Prophet's death, the question of choosing a new leader, or *caliph*, for the Muslim community, or *Ummah*, arose. Initially, his successors could be drawn from the Prophet's contemporaries, but with time, this was no longer possible. Those who became the Shia held that any leader of the Ummah must be a direct descendant of the Prophet; those who became the Sunni argued that lineal descent was not required if the candidate met other standards of faith and knowledge. After bloody struggles, the Sunni became (and remain) the majority sect. (The Shia are dominant in Iran.) The Caliphate—the institutionalized leadership of the Ummah—thus was a Sunni institution that continued until 1924, first under Arab and eventually under Ottoman Turkish control.[90]

It is important to remember that no matter what stream of Islam a person follows, the Koran is his holy book. Because the Koran contains so many verses extolling jihad and otherwise promoting violence, every Muslim of every sect is vulnerable to extremist propaganda, because Islamic radicals can always point to the Koran as their authority. Radical Shiites, radical Sunnis, Wahabists, members of the Muslim Brotherhood—all are able to point to the Koran as the pure path of religious devotion and the rationale behind the violence they espouse.

Bin Laden, in particular, has been able to convince his followers that true Muslims will take up arms in the service of God against Satan:

> Despite his claims to universal leadership, Bin Ladin [*sic*] offers an extreme view of Islamic history designed to appeal mainly to Arabs and Sunnis. He draws on fundamentalists who blame the eventual destruction of the Caliphate on leaders who abandoned the pure path of religious devotion. He repeatedly calls on his followers to embrace martyrdom since "the walls of oppression and humiliation cannot be demolished except in a rain of bullets." For those yearning for a lost sense of order in an older, more tranquil world, he offers his "Caliphate" as an imagined alternative to today's uncertainty. For others, he offers simplistic conspiracies to explain their world.

> Bin Ladin [*sic*] also relies heavily on the Egyptian writer Sayyid Qutb. A member of the Muslim Brotherhood executed in 1966 on charges of attempting to overthrow the government, Qutb mixed Islamic scholarship with a very superficial acquaintance with Western history and thought. Sent by the Egyptian government to study in the United States in the late 1940s, Qutb returned with an enormous loathing of Western society and history. He dismissed Western achievements as entirely material, arguing that Western society possesses "nothing that will satisfy its own conscience and justify its existence."

> Three basic themes emerge from Qutb's writings. First, he claimed that the world was beset with barbarism, licentiousness, and unbelief (a condition he called *jahiliyya*, the religious term for the period of ignorance prior to the revelations given to the Prophet Mohammed). Qutb argued that humans can choose only between Islam and

jahiliyya. Second, he warned that more people, including Muslims, were attracted to jahiliyya and its material comforts than to his view of Islam; jahiliyya could therefore triumph over Islam. Third, no middle ground exists in what Qutb conceived as a struggle between God and Satan. All Muslims—as he defined them—therefore must take up arms in this fight. Any Muslim who rejects his ideas is just one more nonbeliever worthy of destruction.[91]

## Saudi Arabia

Writing in The Washington Post, Youssef Michel Ibrahim said that "There are people inside the American defense establishment -- the most powerful, technologically sophisticated military in the history of mankind -- who believe that the greatest threat they face today may come from followers of an early 18th century religious extremist who called for a renewal of Islamic spirit, moral cleansing and the stripping away of all innovations to Islam since the seventh century. Those disciples are known as Wahabis."[92]

In a November 2003 hearing of the United States Commission on International Religious Freedom, Commission chairman Michael Young had some very strong words about Wahabism and the consequent lack of religious freedom in Saudi Arabia:

Simply put, there is no religious freedom in Saudi Arabia, as both our commission and the Department of State have said in various reports on Saudi Arabia. The Saudi government forcefully and completely limits the public practice or expression of religion to a narrow religious ideology commonly known in the West as Wahabiism. Consequently, non-Wahabi Sunnis, Shi'as, Sufis, and other Muslim groups, as well as the more then 2 million Christians, Hindu and other non-Muslim foreign workers who do not adhere to the Saudi government's interpretation are subject to severe freedom religion violations. Underlying this very restrictive policy on religious freedom is an education system, which contains offensive and discriminatory material in its religious curriculum that is mandatory for all Saudis in public schools.

Our commission has devoted a substantial amount of attention to Saudi Arabia, both before and after the events of September 11th. As we looked at Saudi Arabia, another issue has emerged that appears to flow directly from intolerant and repressive policies within the country. Since September 11th, there have been a growing number of reports that funding coming from Saudi Arabia has been used to finance religious schools and other activities that are alleged to support the kind of hate, intolerance and in some cases violence practiced by Islamic militants and extremists in several parts of the world.

These reports raise troubling questions about the Saudi government's role in propagating worldwide an ideology that is incompatible with both the war against terrorism as well as internationally recognized guarantees of the right to freedom of religion or belief. We ourselves have tried to track at least the number of allegations that have been made as to which countries it is spreading into, and the country count at this point is somewhat over 27.

The conditions inside Saudi Arabia as well as the possibility that the Saudi government has played a role in spreading hatred and intolerance against both Muslims and non-Muslims have very significant implications for US foreign policy. Unfortunately, advancing human rights, including religious freedom, has not been a public feature of the US-Saudi relationship. The commission has recommended that it should be.

For several years, the commission has recommended that successive US administrations designate Saudi Arabia a country of particular concern, which is its statutory designation under the International Religious Freedom Act, required in cases where a country engages in egregious, systematic, and ongoing abuses of religious freedom. A country of particular concern, or CPC designation, is an important diplomatic tool to put the issue of respect for freedom of religion and other human rights on the agenda of the bilateral relationship. Sanctions are an option following CPC designation but not the only option and not required.

To date, the State Department has not designated Saudi Arabia. We ask how a country where religious freedom does not exist at all could possibly fail to qualify for CPC designation. The commission has also recommended that human rights assistance, public diplomacy and other programs and initiatives directed at the Middle East be expanded to include components specifically for Saudi Arabia.

While addressing conditions inside Saudi Arabia, the U.S. government should not turn a blind eye to the question of global exportation of intolerance. In that regard, the commission has recommended that the Congress fund a study to determine whether and how and to the extent to which the Saudi government, members of the royal family or Saudi-funded individuals or institutions are propagating globally a religious ideology that explicitly promotes hate and violence toward members of other religious groups, including disfavored Muslims.[93]

Michael Young asked how a country where religious freedom does not exist at all could possibly fail to qualify for CPC designation. If you've read this far, I'm sure you'll agree that the answer is that too many people and organizations owe favors to the Saudis in return for Saudi petrodollars. Designated or not, Saudi Arabia is a country where Wahabism rules, while other religions and other forms of Islam are not tolerated.

# Iran

Iran's President Mahmoud Ahmadinejad has gotten so much press since he was elected that it's easy to forget the Iran's Supreme Leader is chief cleric Ayatollah Ali Khameni.

Iran has the second-largest reserves of crude oil after Saudi Arabia and the second-largest reserves of natural gas after Russia and has the potential to increase its oil and gas exports greatly.[94] In order to exploit these assets, however, Iran needs capital. At this writing, it remains to be seen whether Iran will get this capital from Russia, from China, from other Islamic states or from the West.

In its background note on Iran, the US Department of State Bureau of Near Eastern Affairs says this:

> Iran's post-revolution difficulties have included an 8-year war with Iraq, internal political struggles and unrest, and economic disorder. The early days of the regime were characterized by severe human rights violations and political turmoil, including the seizure of the U.S. Embassy compound and its occupants on November 4, 1979, by Iranian militants.
>
> By mid-1982, a succession of power struggles eliminated first the center of the political spectrum and then the leftists, leaving only the clergy. There has been some moderation of excesses internally, but Iran still has a serious human rights problem. ***Internationally, Iran remains a major state sponsor of terrorism*** [emphasis added].[95]

Human rights monitors are particularly concerned about the situation of members of the Bahai faith, the largest religious minority in Iran. According to a June 1, 2006, *New York Times* article by Laurie Goodstein, "Members of the Bahai religious minority in Iran said this week that the government had recently intensified a campaign of arrests, raids and propaganda that was aimed at eradicating their religion in Iran, the country of its birth."[96] According to Ms. Goodstein, "The developments have alarmed human rights monitors at the United Nations, who say that since December, the government newspaper in Tehran has published more than 30 articles denigrating the Bahai faith -- even accusing Bahais of sacrificing Muslim children on holy days."[97] An article on the BBC website explains that "Bahá'ís are considered heretics by Muslims because Bahá'u'lláh denied that Muhammad was the last prophet and claimed that he, Bahá'u'lláh, was the latest prophet of God. This denies one of the most fundamental Islamic beliefs."[98]

# Egypt

According to the FBI:

In the aftermath of the [first] World Trade Center bombing, U.S. law enforcement uncovered the plot to bomb several high-profile sites in New York City, including the United Nations building, 26 Federal Plaza (which houses the New York offices of the FBI), and the Lincoln and Holland tunnels. One of the subjects convicted in this conspiracy, Shaykh Omar Abdel Rahman, is the spiritual leader of an Egyptian-based terrorist organization with a worldwide infrastructure. The magnitude of this plot served to reinforce the unsettling reality that international terrorists threaten the United States internally and that U.S. persons and property are a direct target of this activity. Since Shaykh Rahman's imprisonment in 1995 (he is serving a life sentence in federal prison), his followers have threatened to conduct acts of terrorism against Americans to force the U.S. Government to release him.[99]

The Muslim Brotherhood (MB) also known as Al-Ikhwan was founded in Egypt in 1928 by Hassan al-Banna. Like many Islamists, he objected to Western influences and called for a return to the original teachings of Islam. Members and supporters of the Muslim Brotherhood founded al Qaeda.

A Front Page article by Dr. Rachel Ehrenfeld and Alyssa A. Lappen quotes Juan Zarate, the Deputy Assistant to the President and Deputy National Security Advisor for Combating Terrorism as saying, "the Muslim Brotherhood is a group that worries us not because it deals with philosophical or ideological ideas but because it defends the use of violence against civilians."[100] In fact, The MB 1982 secret plan, the Project, instructs all members locally and globally "To channel thought, education and action in order to establish an Islamic power [government] on the earth."[101]

Mohammad Mahdi Akef, the current leader of the MB, has stated that "the Muslim Brotherhood is a global movement whose members cooperate with each other throughout the world, based on the same religious worldview - the spread of Islam, until it rules the world."[102]

## Syria

Syria differs from many Muslim nations in that it is ruled by the Baathist party, a radical but secular Arab nationalist political party. (The Baathists also ruled Iraq briefly in 1963 and then again from July 1968 until 2003.) Its mostly secular ideology contrasts with the theocratic Islamist governments of other Arab countries. Baathist beliefs include Arab Socialism, nationalism, and Pan-Arabism. Syria is a secular, rather than a theocratic dictatorship and is mentioned here because of its support of terrorism. According to the Council on Foreign Relations:

> Syria—along with Iran—gives the Lebanese militia Hezbollah "substantial amounts of financial, training, weapons, explosives, political, diplomatic, and organizational aid," according to the State

Department. Iranian arms bound for Hezbollah regularly pass through Syria, experts say. Syria, which has effectively occupied and controlled neighboring Lebanon since 1990, has also let Hezbollah operate in Lebanon and attack Israel, often ratcheting up regional tensions.

More recently, the United States accuses Syria of letting militants, who support the Iraqi insurgency, easily pass through its border with Iraq. In September 2004, Syria hosted border security discussions with the Iraqis and adopted a number of measures, but U.S. officials feel more needs to be done to prevent terrorists from taking advantage of the Syrian border with Iraq.

Syria has also provided training, weapons, safe haven, and logistical support to both leftist and Islamist Palestinian hard-liners. The far-left Popular Front for the Liberation of Palestine-General Command and the fundamentalist Palestinian Islamic Jihad have their headquarters in Damascus, and other terrorist groups, including the Islamist group Hamas and the leftist Popular Front for the Liberation of Palestine, maintain offices there.

From 1980 until 1998, the Kurdistan Workers' Party, which sought an independent Kurdish state, used Syria as a headquarters and base of operations against neighboring Turkey.[103]

# Countries with a Large Muslim Population

*Except where otherwise noted, statistics are taken from The World Factbook (http://www.cia.gov/cia/publications/factbook/)*

| Country | Religion |
| --- | --- |
| Afghanistan | Sunni Muslim 80%, Shia Muslim 19%, other 1% "Virtually the entire population is Muslim. Between 80 and 85 percent of Muslims are Sunni and 15 to 19 percent, Shia. The minority Shia are economically |

| Country | Religion |
|---------|----------|
|  | disadvantaged and frequently subjected to discrimination. Small numbers of Hindus and Sikhs live in urban centers. A Jewish population that numbered 5,000 in 1948 had left Afghanistan entirely by 2000."[104] |
| Algeria | Sunni Muslim (state religion) 99%, Christian and Jewish 1% "The country's decade-long civil conflict pitted self-proclaimed radical Muslims belonging to the Armed Islamic Group and its later offshoot, the Salafist Group for Preaching and Combat, against moderate Muslims. While estimates vary, approximately 100,000 to 150,000 civilians, terrorists, and security forces have been killed during the past 13 years. Radical Islamic extremists have issued public threats against all "infidels" in the country, both foreigners and citizens, and have killed both Muslims and non-Muslims, including missionaries."[105] |
| Bahrain | Muslim (Shia and Sunni) 81.2%, Christian 9%, other 9.8% (2001 census) "Muslim citizens belong to the Shia and Sunni branches of Islam, with Shia constituting as much as two-thirds of the indigenous population. "[106] |
| Bangladesh | Muslim 83%, Hindu 16%, other 1% (1998) |
| Chad | Muslim 51%, Christian 35%, animist 7%, other 7% "The vast majority of Muslims are adherents of a moderate branch of mystical Islam (Sufism) known locally as Tidjani, which originated in 1727 under Sheik Ahmat Tidjani in present-day Morocco and Algeria. Tidjani Islam, as practiced in the country, incorporates some local African religious elements. A small minority of the country's Muslims (5 to 10 percent) is considered fundamentalist."[107] |
| China | Muslim 1%-2% (1% would be over 13 *million* Chinese Muslims) |
| Comoros | Sunni Muslim 98%, Roman Catholic 2% |
| Djibouti | Muslim 94%, Christian 6% |

| Country | Religion |
|---|---|
| Egypt | Muslim (mostly Sunni) 90%, Coptic 9%, other Christian 1% |
| Eritrea | Muslim, Coptic Christian, Roman Catholic, Protestant |
| Ethiopia | Muslim 45%-50%, Ethiopian Orthodox 35%-40%, animist 12%, other 3%-8% |
| India | Hindu 80.5%, Muslim 13.4%, Christian 2.3%, Sikh 1.9%, other 1.8%, unspecified 0.1% (2001 census) |
| Indonesia | Muslim 88%, Protestant 5%, Roman Catholic 3%, Hindu 2%, Buddhist 1%, other 1% (1998) |
| Iran | Shia Muslim 89%, Sunni Muslim 9%, Zoroastrian, Jewish, Christian, and Baha'i 2% |
| Iraq | Muslim 97% (Shia 60%-65%, Sunni 32%-37%), Christian or other 3% |
| Jordan | Sunni Muslim 92%, Christian 6% (majority Greek Orthodox, but some Greek and Roman Catholics, Syrian Orthodox, Coptic Orthodox, Armenian Orthodox, and Protestant denominations), other 2% (several small Shia Muslim and Druze populations) (2001 est.) |
| Kuwait | Muslim 85% (Sunni 70%, Shia 30%), Christian, Hindu, Parsi, and other 15% |
| Kazakhstan | Muslim 47%, Russian Orthodox 44%, Protestant 2%, other 7% |
| Lebanon | Muslim 59.7% (Shia, Sunni, Druze, Isma'ilite, Alawite or Nusayri), Christian 39% (Maronite Catholic, Greek Orthodox, Melkite Catholic, Armenian Orthodox, Syrian Catholic, Armenian Catholic, Syrian Orthodox, Roman Catholic, Chaldean, Assyrian, Copt, Protestant), other 1.3% |
| Libya | Sunni Muslim 97% |
| Mali | Muslim 90%, indigenous beliefs 9%, Christian 1% |
| Maldives | Sunni Muslim |
| Mauritania | Muslim 100% |
| Mayotte | Muslim 97%, Christian (mostly Roman Catholic) |
| Morocco | Muslim 98.7%, Christian 1.1%, Jewish 0.2% |

| Country | Religion |
|---|---|
| Niger | Muslim 80%, remainder indigenous beliefs and Christian |
| Nigeria | Muslim 50%, Christian 40%, indigenous beliefs 10% |
| Oman | Ibadhi Muslim 75%, Sunni Muslim, Shia Muslim, Hindu |
| Pakistan | Muslim 97% (Sunni 77%, Shia 20%), Christian, Hindu, and other 3% |
| Palestinian Authority | Islam is the de facto approved religion; 38,000 Christian Palestinians in the West Bank and Gaza are treated as second-class citizens; and no law protects freedom of religion (source: www.discoverthenetwork.com) |
| Qatar | Muslim 95% |
| Saudi Arabia | Muslim 100% |
| Somalia | Sunni Muslim |
| Sudan | Sunni Muslim 70% (in north), indigenous beliefs 25%, Christian 5% (mostly in south and Khartoum) |
| Syria | Sunni Muslim 74%, Alawite, Druze, and other Muslim sects 16%, Christian (various sects) 10%, Jewish (tiny communities in Damascus, Al Qamishli, and Aleppo) "Though three quarters of Syria's population are Sunni, the ruling party has long drawn its leaders from the minority Alawi sect, an offshoot of Shiite Islam, which - along with Druze and other Muslim sects - makes up just 16 percent of the national population. Pan-Arab and secular, the Baath Party has historically ruled on a domestic platform of protecting the rights of Syria's minorities."[108] |
| Tunisia | Muslim 98%, Christian 1%, Jewish and other 1% |
| Turkey | Muslim 99.8% (mostly Sunni), other 0.2% (mostly Christians and Jews) |
| Turkmenistan | Muslim 89%, Eastern Orthodox 9%, unknown 2% |
| U.A.E. | Muslim 96% (Shia 16%), Christian, Hindu, and other 4% |
| Uzbekistan | Muslim 88% (mostly Sunnis), Eastern Orthodox 9%, other 3% |
| Western | Muslim |

| Country | Religion |
|---------|----------|
| Sahara | |
| Yemen | Muslim including Shaf'i (Sunni) and Zaydi (Shia), small numbers of Jewish, Christian, and Hindu |

# CHAPTER 9

# DID SADDAM HAVE WEAPONS OF MASS DESTRUCTION?

If you're still wondering whether Saddam had WMDs, the short answer is a resounding *yes*. The existence of Saddam's WMDs has been confirmed by a number of reliable sources.

In "Iraqi WMD Mystery Solved," Jamie Glazov of *Front Page Magazine* interviewed geopolitical analyst Ryan Mauro about audiotapes recently released by the Intelligence Summit, a non-profit forum that brings together the intelligence agencies of the free world and emerging democracies. In these tapes, Saddam Hussein and his key officials are heard discussing their WMD programs. Because Mauro had written a book (*Death to America: The Unreported Battle of Iraq*) claiming that Russia helped move Iraqi WMD into Syria, Glazov asked Mauro how the tapes squared with Mauro's claim. Mauro replied:

> The tapes are extremely significant in that they prove, beyond a shadow of a doubt, that as of the year 2000, Saddam Hussein had a secret plasma program to enrich uranium for nuclear weapons, or "special bombs" as he calls them. The Duelfer

Report previously concluded that this type of enrichment program ended in the 1980s, but here we have Saddam and his top advisors discussing using a power plant in the area of Basra for the program. The scientists involved in the program are not known to the UN, leaving Western intelligence clueless.

On the tapes, you hear Saddam discussing the assistance of Russia and Brazil in dealing with the United Nations. He laughs off inspections, as his son-in-law who later defects, Hussein Kamil, reports how as late as 1995 their chemical and biological programs were being hidden from the world. They also discuss keeping the ingredients for these weapons separate, so that should they be found, they will be looked at as innocent dual-use items. They were not destroyed in 1991 as the Duelfer Report concludes. There are even indications on the tapes that Iraq may have had a role in the 2001 anthrax attacks.[109]

These are not by any means the only evidences that Saddam's WMDs did, in fact, exist. General Georges Sada was one of Saddam Hussein's top military advisors—a devout Christian known for telling the truth, even when the truth was dangerous. In his book, *Saddam's Secrets*, General Sada gives his own eyewitness account of Saddam's use of WMDs, as well as the various ways in which Saddam hid WMDs from various inspection teams.

There is both good news and bad news in what General Sada has to say: the good news is that Saddam had not produced or acquired any nuclear warheads that could actually be deployed against an enemy. The bad news was that Saddam did of course have and use biological and chemical WMDs.

General Sada writes:

Saddam was committed to using WMDs and he wouldn't hesitate to use them on his enemies. The level of expertise among scientists who were developing our nuclear weapons systems was very high, but it was difficult to acquire the specialized equipment that was needed for weapons development. So while he had plans—Saddam had set very ambitious goals for the nuclear engineers— we weren't as far along in the nuclear program as we were with biological and chemical weapons. But we were very sophisticated with those, and we had plenty of them.[110]

About nuclear weapons, General Sada goes on to say:

I learned in 2005, that Saddam had even made arrangements with a group of nuclear scientists in China to produce nuclear arms for him overseas. At least $5 million changed hands at that time, and as late as 1992 these plans were apparently still ongoing. But to my knowledge our own scientists had not yet produced—or acquired by other means— any nuclear warheads that could actually be deployed against an enemy.[111]

Speaking from his own experience in the field, General Sada had this to say about chemical WMDs:

It's important to understand, particularly in light of all the controversy of recent months, that Iraq did have weapons of mass destruction both before and after 1991, and I can assure you they were used. They were used on our own people. They were used in artillery shells, cannons, and by aerial dispersion of toxins by both helicopters and fixed-wing aircraft against Saddam's enemies. And this was always done in a particular way. Whenever we received ops orders to attack using WMDs, the orders never said, "Okay, use WMDs on this one." Instead they said, "Special mission with special weapons," and the commanders all knew what that meant.

I'm certain that many of those ops orders were recovered later by coalition forces after liberation in 2003, although intelligence officers may not have known what those words, written in Arabic, actually meant. But let me be very clear: in every case, "Special mission with special weapons" meant that the field commanders were to use chemical weapons to attack the enemy.[112]

General Sada goes on to give a fascinating account of how many WMDs were actually flown to Syria disguised as humanitarian aid in the wake of a flood caused by the collapse of an irrigation dam. Saddam used civilian 747 and 727 airplanes to fly fifty-six sorties to Syria, where they were handed over to ordnance specialists who promised to hold the weapons for as long as necessary. The plans for the weapons transfers were put together by "Ali and Ali." The Iraqi Ali was Ali Hussein al-Majid (Chemical Ali); the Syrian Ali was General Abu Ali, a cousin of Syrian president Bashar Al-Assad.

According to General Sada:

To keep all these illegal transfers under wraps, the two Ali's worked through a false company called SES. This company played a key role in transporting equipment back and forth between Syria and Iraq, as well as in smuggling many former government officials out of Iraq prior to and immediately after the U.S. invasion in March 2003. These are the same people who had previously organized the illegal sale of oil, natural gas, gasoline, sulfate, and other resources produced in Iraq to countries in the region, defying United Nations sanctions.[113]

A reference to these events can be found on FinancialTimes.com in an article entitled "Dutch daily says Iraq hid weapons of mass destruction in Syria."

The Netherlands De Telegraaf daily says it possesses a letter and a map showing that Iraq has concealed its weapons of mass destruction in Syria. A senior Syrian intelligence officer allegedly gave detailed information to a Syrian journalist in exile, who in turn passed on the information to the [Netherlands] daily last Saturday [3 January].

At a meeting in a Paris cafe, dissident journalist Nizar Nayyouf, who received the UNESCO press freedom award in 2000, showed the exact locations of the weapons. Nayyouf is convinced that the United States knows about these arms stores, but that it is reluctant to release this news for political reasons. In his opinion, the United States does not yet want to get rid of the Syrian regime." Obviously, as soon as the United States makes up its mind or wants to oust the Syrian rulers, it will release the discovery of these arms stores as a major scoop."[114]

General Sada isn't the only former Iraqi general to verify the existence of Iraqi WMDs. In a transcript of testimony by former Iraqi General Ibrahim Al-Tikriti, Tikriti says:

I was formerly known as Iraqi Fedayeen Major General, Ali Ibrahim Al-Tikriti. I was one of Saddam's chief Generals dealing with his secret nuclear, chemical, and biological programs. ...

As far as the weapons inspections were concerned we devised very lucrative measures to hide our ongoing nuclear projects. For instance we were under strict orders to destroy all materials, memos, and reports pertaining to such projects. Immediately after completion of the orders, we were also given orders at random to abandon nuclear facilities and sites where nuclear, chemical, or biological research was being conducted and to move them to future facilities that were not known about until the materials were ready for transport. Many of the workers used for such transport were immediately purged as to leave few witnesses.

As for foreign involvement in our programs, much of this can be attributed to the Russian Federation. Moscow directed many programs around the world, Iraq being one of them where chemical weapons and scientists were sent to further develop unconventional munitions. Contingency plans were developed though, in the event that the host nation was compromised, as in the case of the 2003 invasion of Iraq. Spetsnaz forces were sent to retrieve the munitions as well as any materials related to Russian involvement. These programs were designed to build stronger relations with countries that were discordant with the west.[115]

Reports of WMDs being stockpiled, whether in Iraq or elsewhere in the Arab world, are especially disturbing because as long as these weapons exist, they have the potential of being used. Weapons still in Iraq could be used by Iraqis. Weapons that were transferred to Syria could be used by the Syrians. And weapons cached anywhere in the Muslim world could potentially be used by whichever Islamic terrorists are favored by their custodians.

In testimony before the House International Relations Committee, John R. Bolton, Under Secretary for Arms Control and International Security had this to say about Syria:

Syria remains a security concern on two important counts: terrorism and weapons of mass destruction. I will focus on the latter, although the potential linkages are obvious. Specifically, our Coalition's operations in Iraq showed that this Administration and the international community take the link between terrorism and WMD [weapons of mass destruction] most seriously. There is no graver threat to our country today than states that both sponsor terrorism and possess or aspire to possess weapons of mass destruction. Syria, which offers physical sanctuary and political protection to groups such as Hizballah, HAMAS, and Palestinian Islamic Jihad, and whose terrorist operations have killed hundreds of innocent people – including Americans - - falls into this category of states of potential dual threat. While there is currently no information indicating that the Syrian Government has transferred WMD to terrorist organizations or would permit such groups to acquire them, Syria's ties to numerous terrorist groups underlie the reasons for our continued anxiety. [116]

General Sada himself tells us that Saddam hid large caches of weapons in order to keep them from the United Nations inspectors.

Large stockpiles of weapons were destroyed by the United Nations weapons inspectors between 1991 and 2003, but I can assure you they never got them all. There were tons of raw material, shells and shell casings, rockets and grenades, both half-completed and fully completed devices hidden in large caches. In 2001 and then again in 2002, Saddam called a meeting of all the top scientists, researchers and technicians involved in developing weapons systems, and he told them to memorize their plans. Before the paper trail was destroyed linking Saddam to these plans he made certain, on the threat of death and dismemberment, that every single plan and every schematic was committed to memory. [117]

In point of fact, while US forces were unable to find WMDs hidden in Iraq, this doesn't mean that they haven't found other stockpiled weapons. Many internet sites have posted pictures of a US military search team uncovering MiG-25 and Su-25 ground attack jets that were found buried at al-Taqqadum airfield west of

Baghdad. The pictures on the following pages come from the official United States Department of Defense photos website.

*US forces use heavy equipment to pull a MiG-25R Foxbat-B from beneath the sands in Iraq on July 6, 2003. DoD photo Master Sgt. T. Collins, US Air Force.[118]*

This report comes from the BBC:

US forces in Iraq have discovered dozens of Iraqi fighter aircraft buried in the desert, US officials have said.

A Pentagon official told the Associated Press news agency that several MiG-25s and Su-25 attack planes were found hidden at al-Taqqadum air base west of Baghdad.

The planes were unearthed by teams hunting for alleged weapons of mass destruction.[119]

The same incident was also reported in a United States

Department of Defense news release:

*A US military search team uncovers a MiG-25R Foxbat-B from beneath the sands in Iraq on July 6, 2003. Several MiG-25s and Su-25 aircraft have been found buried at Al-Taqqadum airfield west of Baghdad. DoD photo Master Sgt. T. Collins, US Air Force.[120]*

WASHINGTON, Aug. 6, 2003 -- American forces have found Russian fighter jets buried in the Iraqi desert, Defense Secretary Donald Rumsfeld said in an Aug. 5 press briefing.

"We'd heard a great many things had been buried, but we had not known where they were, and we'd been operating in that immediate vicinity for weeks and weeks and weeks ... 12, 13 weeks, and didn't know they were (there)," Rumsfeld said.

The secretary said he wasn't sure how many such aircraft had been found, but noted, "It wasn't one or two."

He said it's a "classic example" of the challenges the Iraqi Survey Group is facing in finding weapons of mass destruction in the country.

"Something as big as an airplane that's within … a stone's throw of where you're functioning, and you don't know it's there because you don't run around digging into everything on a discovery process," Rumsfeld explained. "So until you find somebody who tells you where to look, or until nature clears some sand away and exposes something over time, we're simply not going to know.

"But, as we all know," he added, "the absence of evidence is not evidence of absence."[121]

NewsMax.com has this to add about the buried airplanes:

Contrary to what some in the major media have reported, not all the jets found were from the Gulf War era.

The Russian-made MiG-25 Foxbat being recovered by U.S. Air Force troops in the photos is an advanced reconnaissance version never before seen in the West and is equipped with sophisticated electronic warfare devices.[122]

Did Saddam Hussein have and use weapons of mass destruction? He most certainly did. Do they still pose a threat to us? They most certainly do. Ironically, it's not the still-hidden stockpiles that need worry us the most—it's the ones Saddam entrusted into other Muslim hands. It is those WMDs that could be used against us at any time.

## Should the United States Have Attacked Iraq?

The American press has made much of the fact that we have been unable to find WMDs stockpiled in Iraq, and has been using the lack of any evidence of WMD stockpiles to say that we were wrong to invade Iraq. However, given the fact that it is part of the jihadist mindset to attack its enemies when those enemies are perceived as weak, I believe we were right to attack Iraq.

Speaking at Princeton on the occasion of George Kennan's 100th birthday, Secretary of State Colin L. Powell said:

> U.S. policies over many administrations have reassured friends and allies that they don't need to pursue their own nuclear weapons, especially if they're in alliance with the United States and we can make sure that they will be protected against the threats that might be out there. We have been able to persuade others that the potential costs of acquiring such weapons would be outweighed by just the trouble they get themselves into. There are no benefits to these weapons compared to the cost that is paid to acquire them.
>
> That's why the leaderships of most countries have come to see that weapons of mass destruction won't make them safer, won't contribute to their building a vibrant economy, and won't exactly help either their international image either, or their relationship with the United States of America.
>
> And after all, nearly every government, every nation, wants good relations with the United States. But not all. I wish it were all.[123]

Later in that same speech, Powell went on to speak about the work of Dr. David Kay, whom he called "our chief investigator in this matter [WMDs]." Dr. Kay at the time was Director of Central Intelligence George J. Tenet's Special Advisor for Strategy regarding Iraqi Weapons of Mass Destruction (WMD) Programs.

> Whatever you heard about Dr. Kay's work about the stockpile, this is also what Dr. Kay has said. He found in Iraq a regime that, in his words, "was in clear violation of UN Resolution 1441," that

"maintained WMD programs and activities," and that "clearly had the intention to resume their programs."

And Dr. Kay connected some dots out of all of this, dots he connected on his own: "we know that terrorists were passing through Iraq. And we know now that there was little control over Iraq's weapons capabilities. I think it shows," he said, "Iraq was a dangerous place...I actually think this may be one of those cases where it was even more dangerous than we thought."

His conclusion: "I personally believe the war was justified."

It was justified....Not only have coalition forces rid the world of a regime that was simultaneously building palaces for its pampered and digging mass graves for its innocents, the object lesson of the war has led to some important successes in the non-proliferation area. So don't let anybody be confused by the debates that are going on. America did the right thing. [124]

In the title of this chapter I ask, "Did Saddam have Weapons of Mass Destruction? The answer seems to be that yes, he had them—and he got rid of them. As we have seen, he shipped them to Syria using civilian 747 and 727 airplanes.

In a *New York Sun* article entitled "He Lied So Often, No One Believed He Removed WMD," reporter Daniel Pipes said, "The great mystery of the 2003 war in Iraq - "What about the WMD?" has finally been resolved. The short answer is: Saddam Hussein's persistent record of lying meant no one believed him when he at the last moment actually removed the weapons of mass destruction."[125] Pipes' conclusion? "Coalition intelligence agencies, not surprisingly, missed the final and unexpected twist in a long-running drama. Neither those agencies nor Western politicians lied; Saddam was the evil impostor whose deceptions in the end confused and endangered everyone, including himself.[126]

*PART 2—A BIBLICAL PERSPECTIVE*

# CHAPTER 10

# WHAT ABOUT ISRAEL?

Charles Krauthammer tells us that "Israel is the very embodiment of Jewish continuity: It is the only nation on earth that inhabits the same land, bears the same name, speaks the same language, and worships the same God that it did 3,000 years ago. You dig the soil and you find pottery from Davidic times, coins from Bar Kokhba, and 2,000-year-old scrolls written in a script remarkably like the one that today advertises ice cream at the corner candy store."[127]

For centuries, the continued existence of the Jewish people was considered by many to be proof of God's existence. Today you could say the same for the Nation of Israel. In 2 Chronicles 6:6, God said, "But I have chosen Jerusalem, that my name might be there ..."

Both Jews and Christians believe the land of Israel was given to the Jewish people by God Himself: "For all the land which thou seest, to thee will I give it, and to thy seed for ever" Genesis 13:15 (KJV).

Unless you understand what the Bible has to say about the Jews, Jerusalem, and the nation of Israel, you cannot understand what is happing—and what is going to happen—in the Middle East.

For over 3,000 years, since Israel first became a nation around 1200 BC, Jews have regarded the Land of Israel as their homeland. Jews and Christians alike refer to it as "The Holy Land"—the location where the Bible events took place.

The Apostle Luke, writing in the Book of Acts, said

> The former treatise have I made, O Theophilus, of all that Jesus began both to do and teach, Until the day in which he was taken up, after that he through the Holy Ghost had given commandments unto the apostles whom he had chosen: To whom also he showed himself alive after his passion by many infallible proofs, being seen of them forty days, and speaking of the things pertaining to the kingdom of God:
>
> Acts 1:1-3

New Testament believers needed proof that the Gospel was true, and God gave them "many infallible proofs." People today are no different. We need to know that God is real and the Bible is true. Some people have taught that you have to take "a leap of faith" to believe in God, but the Bible contains so many prophecies that have already been fulfilled—many in modern times—that we too have been provided with "many infallible proofs."

If you want proof that God exists and His Word is true, all you need to do is to look at the history of the Jewish people. Even before the birth of the modern State of Israel, the very existence of the Jewish people was seen as proof of the existence of God:

> Said Mark Twain, "The Egyptians, the Babylonians, and the Persian rose, filled the planet with sound and splendour, and faded to dream stuff and passed away. The Greeks and Romans followed and made a vast noise and they are gone. Other peoples have sprung up and held their torch high for

a time. But it burned out, and they sit in twilight now, or have vanished. . . ."

When Napoleon, campaigning in Eastern Europe, asked one of his advisors to show him a miracle, the advisor said, "The Jews." When Queen Victoria, long in mourning for her beloved Prince Albert, asked Disraeli in her despair if he knew of any proof of the existence of God, all he said was, "The Jews."[128]

Even as late as the first part of the twentieth century, most people thought that the Jews were so dispersed that it would be impossible for them to become a nation ever again. After all, they didn't have a homeland and they didn't have an army. They didn't even have a common language. Until the Zionist movement—and really not until the birth of the nation of Israel—Hebrew was a dead language. Scholars and rabbis were able to read Hebrew, but nobody used it as their native tongue. But even though the reestablishment of the state of Israel looked impossible, God had promised that just as He brought Israel out of Egypt, He would bring the children of Israel back to their homeland once again.

> Therefore, behold, the days come, saith the LORD, that it shall no more be said, The LORD liveth, that brought up the children of Israel out of the land of Egypt; But, The LORD liveth, that brought up the children of Israel from the land of the north, and from all the lands whither he had driven them: and I will bring them again into their land that I gave unto their fathers. Behold, I will send for many fishers, saith the LORD, and they shall fish them; and after will I send for many hunters, and they shall hunt them from every mountain, and from every hill, and out of the holes of the rocks.
>
> Jeremiah 16:14-16

When Jesus called Peter and Andrew, he said, "Follow me,

and I will make you fishers of men" (Matthew 4:19). Biblically speaking, "fishers" are preachers—people who work through persuasion. Put even more simply, "fishers" are "good guys" who use bait to entice the fish to do their bidding. What about the "hunters"? Unfortunately, the hunters are the bad guys.

In the 19$^{th}$ century, Palestine (not yet called Israel) was a part of the Ottoman Empire. In the late 1870s, Jewish philanthropists ("good guys") sponsored agricultural settlements for Russian Jews in Palestine. A small group of immigrants from Russia arrived in Palestine in 1882. In Zionist history, this has become known as the First Aliyah—aliyah being a Hebrew word meaning 'ascent' and referring to the act of "ascending" to the Holy Land. From then until World War II, many Zionists "fished" for Jews who would be willing to emigrate to Palestine. Then came World War II and the "hunters." During the Holocaust, the Nazis hunted the Jews "from every mountain, and from every hill, and out of the holes of the rocks" in fulfillment of God's prophetic Word.

It is interesting that Ezekiel prophesied that we would say, "The LORD liveth, that brought up the children of Israel *from the land of the north*, [emphasis added] and from all the lands whither he had driven them," because that this is exactly what happened. The First Aliyah was from Russia—the land of the north. After that, God also brought Jews to Israel "from all the lands whither he had driven them." As there are still many Jews living outside of Israel, this can be considered to be a Biblical work in progress. Nehemiah 1:9 promises, "But if ye turn unto me, and keep my commandments, and do them; though there were of you cast out unto the uttermost part of the heaven, yet will I gather them from thence, and will bring them unto the place that I have chosen to set my name there." (Please note that until the twentieth century space travel was unknown, so the part about "though there were of you cast out unto the uttermost part of the heaven" is *really* prophetic.)

The scripture in Ezekiel is just one of many Bible prophecies that predict the re-gathering of Israel. Ezekiel, Isaiah, Deuteronomy, Amos, Hosea, Jeremiah, Jesus (in Luke 21:24) and

Paul (in Romans 11) all prophesied that God would re-gather the Jewish people. Amos 9:14-15 says, "And I will bring again the captivity of my people of Israel, and they shall build the waste cities, and inhabit *them*; and they shall plant vineyards, and drink the wine thereof; they shall also make gardens, and eat the fruit of them. And I will plant them upon their land, and they shall no more be pulled up out of their land which I have given them, saith the LORD thy God."

Of course, to be gathered, first you have to be scattered, and the Jews had been scattered shortly after the time of Christ. This was itself the fulfillment of many prophecies, including this one by Jesus in Matthew 23:34-38:

> Wherefore, behold, I send unto you prophets, and wise men, and scribes: and *some* of them ye shall kill and crucify; and *some* of them shall ye scourge in your synagogues, and persecute *them* from city to city: That upon you may come all the righteous blood shed upon the earth, from the blood of righteous Abel unto the blood of Zacharias son of Barachias, whom ye slew between the temple and the altar. Verily I say unto you, All these things shall come upon this generation. O Jerusalem, Jerusalem, *thou* that killest the prophets, and stonest them which are sent unto thee, how often would I have gathered thy children together, even as a hen gathereth her chickens under *her* wings, and ye would not! Behold, your house is left unto you desolate.

In the next chapter of Matthew, Jesus prophesied that the Temple was to be destroyed: "And Jesus went out, and departed from the temple: and his disciples came to *him* for to shew him the buildings of the temple. And Jesus said unto them, See ye not all these things? verily I say unto you, There shall not be left here one stone upon another, that shall not be thrown down" Matthew 24:1-2.

Scholars disagree about how long "a generation" is, but we all know of human beings who have lived to be a hundred years old, and it took less than that for Jesus' prophecy to come to pass upon "this generation." In early New Testament times, two Jewish-Roman wars devastated the Land of Israel. The First Jewish-Roman War in 66-73 AD left the Temple destroyed and the land in ruins. This was the fulfillment of Jesus' prophecies about Jerusalem and the Temple.

Sixty years later, the Romans again conquered Israel in a two-year war known as Bar Kokhba's revolt. After Bar Kokhba's revolt, Jerusalem was razed, Jews were forbidden to live there, and a Roman city, Aelia Capitolina, was constructed on the ruins. In order to humiliate what was left of the Jewish population, the Emperor Hadrian changed the name of Judea (the Roman name of the province) to Syria Palaestina. He didn't do this for love of the Palestinians—there were no "Palestinians." Syria Palaestina was named for the *Philistines*, an ancient enemy of the Jews, as a deliberate anti-Semitic gesture. Over the years, the word "Palaestina" eventually became "Palestine," and Palestine was the name used for the Holy Land until modern-day Israel was born.

After the Romans, the land that became modern-day Israel was ruled by Islamic and Christian crusaders, by the Ottoman Empire, and finally by the British Empire. The British defeated the Ottoman Empire in 1917. That same year, British Foreign Secretary Arthur J. Balfour, writing on behalf of the British Cabinet, issued a statement known as the Balfour Declaration, the most important part of which read as follows: "His Majesty's Government view with favour the establishment in Palestine of a national home for the Jewish people, and will use their best endeavours to facilitate the achievement of this object."

The Britain occupied Palestine until the end of World War I. After the war, the Allied powers chose Britain as the administrator of Palestine in an arrangement known as the Palestine Mandate. From then until 1948, the British ruled what was then known as Palestine.

In 1939 the British, in their White Paper of 1939, limited Jewish immigration to 75,000 over the next five years and made it contingent on Arab consent thereafter.  It also restricted land purchases by Jews.  It said in part that "His Majesty's Government therefore now declare unequivocally that it is not part of their policy that Palestine should become a Jewish State."  The Jewish community saw this as a betrayal—and one that came at a time when European Jews desperately needed a homeland they could flee to.  However, the White Paper guided British policy throughout World War II and even afterwards.

In 1947 the British government decided to withdraw from the mandate, and the UN General Assembly approved the 1947 UN Partition Plan, which would divide the Palestinian territory into two states—Israel and Jordan.  Israel tentatively accepted the partition, but the Arab League rejected it.  On May 14, 1948, just before the British Mandate was to expire at midnight on May 15, the State of Israel was proclaimed.

## The Birth of Israel

On May 14, 1948, Ben-Gurion proclaimed the establishment of the State of Israel.  On May 15, Britain relinquished the Mandate at 6:00 P.M. and the United States announced their de facto recognition of Israel.  This is a fulfillment of Isaiah 66:7-8:

> Before she travailed, she brought forth; before her pain came, she was delivered of a man child.  Who hath heard such a thing? who hath seen such things?  Shall the earth be made to bring forth in one day? *or* shall a nation be born at once? for as soon as Zion travailed, she brought forth her children.

*Before* she travailed, Israel became a nation.  Her travail—the Israeli War of Independence—took place *after* she brought forth the nation in a day.

Here is an account of the Israeli War of Independence taken from the www.globalsecurity.org web site:

On May 14, 1948, Ben-Gurion and his associates proclaimed the establishment of the State of Israel. On the following day Britain relinquished the Mandate at 6:00 P.M. and the United States announced de facto recognition of Israel. Soviet recognition was accorded on May 18; by April 1949, fifty-three nations, including Britain, had extended recognition. In May 1949, the UN General Assembly, on recommendation of the Security Council, admitted Israel to the UN.

Meanwhile, Arab military forces began their invasion of Israel on May 15. Initially these forces consisted of approximately 8,000 to 10,000 Egyptians, 2,000 to 4,000 Iraqis, 4,000 to 5,000 Transjordanians, 3,000 to 4,000 Syrians, 1,000 to 2,000 Lebanese, and smaller numbers of Saudi Arabian and Yemeni troops, about 25,000 in all. Israeli forces composed of the Haganah, such irregular units as the Irgun and the Stern Gang, and women's auxiliaries numbered 35,000 or more. By October 14, Arab forces deployed in the war zones had increased to about 55,000, including not more than 5,000 irregulars of Hajj Amin al Husayni's Palestine Liberation Force. The Israeli military forces had increased to approximately 100,000. Except for the British-trained Arab Legion of Transjordan, Arab units were largely ill-trained and inexperienced. Israeli forces, usually operating with interior lines of communication, included an estimated 20,000 to 25,000 European World War II veterans.

By January 1949, Jewish forces held the area that was to define Israel's territory until June 1967, an area that was significantly larger than the area

116

designated by the UN partition plan. The part of Palestine remaining in Arab hands was limited to that held by the Arab Legion of Transjordan and the Gaza area held by Egypt at the cessation of hostilities. The area held by the Arab Legion was subsequently annexed by Jordan and is commonly referred to as the West Bank. Jerusalem was divided. The Old City, the Western Wall and the site of Solomon's Temple, upon which stands the Muslim mosque called the Dome of the Rock, remained in Jordanian hands; the New City lay on the Israeli side of the line. Although the West Bank remained under Jordanian suzerainty until 1967, only two countries-- Britain and Pakistan--granted de jure recognition of the annexation.[129]

Today, a rational, thinking person can see that hundreds of prophecies made in the Old Testament have been fulfilled in the last two thousand years, with many being fulfilled in modern times. If the survival of the Jews as a people was seen by Disraeli as proof that God exists, how much more should the re-establishment of Israel as a nation be seen that God exists and His Word is true?

## Israel's Right to Exist

In February 2006, Hamas leader Mahmoud al-Zahar proclaimed that "Israel is an illegal entity, and no amount of pressure can force us to recognize its right to exist... the western countries can take their aid and go to hell."[130]

I have already mentioned that in New Testament times, there were no Palestinians. In point of fact, the "Palestinians" are a made-up people. The "Palestinians" are simply Arabs, pure and simple. Nobody mentioned Palestinians during the Israeli War of Independence—Jews and Arabs, yes; Palestine, yes; but not Palestinians. "Palestinians" weren't spoken of until 1967, when the Israelis gained control of the West Bank and Old Jerusalem.

Writing in WorldNetDaily, Arab-American journalist

Joseph Farah says:

> Isn't it interesting that prior to the 1967 Arab-Israeli war, there was no serious movement for a Palestinian homeland?

> "Well, Farah," you might say, "that was before the Israelis seized the West Bank and Old Jerusalem."

> That's true. In the Six-Day War, Israel captured Judea, Samaria and East Jerusalem. But they didn't capture these territories from Yasser Arafat. They captured them from Jordan's King Hussein. I can't help but wonder why all these Palestinians suddenly discovered their national identity after Israel won the war. [131]

No matter what the news media would have us believe, the Palestinians are not now—and never have been—a distinct people. In the article quoted above, Farah goes on to say:

> ...There is no language known as Palestinian. There is no distinct Palestinian culture. There has never been a land known as Palestine governed by Palestinians. Palestinians are Arabs, indistinguishable from Jordanians (another recent invention), Syrians, Lebanese, Iraqis, etc. Keep in mind that the Arabs control 99.9 percent of the Middle East lands. Israel represents one-tenth of 1 percent of the landmass.

> But that's too much for the Arabs. They want it all. [132]

Palestinians are Arabs, and until Yasser Arafat came along in the 1970's, no one had heard of a Palestinian "nation." In an article entitled "The truth about Israel, and why Christians should care," Steve Meyers writes:

So where was the Palestinian nation [prior to Yasser Arafat]? It did not exist because it has never existed! If you doubt it, name the Palestinian leader before Yasser Arafat. Before you burst a blood vessel trying, the answer is that there wasn't one, because Arafat invented the word.[133]

According to Dore Gold and Jeff Helmreich, "There was no active movement to form a unique Palestinian state prior to 1967. In 1956, Ahmad Shuqairy, who would found the PLO eight years later, told the UN Security Council: "it is common knowledge that Palestine is nothing but southern Syria."[134] (Greater Syria historically included what is now Lebanon, Israel, the Palestinian Territories, and parts of Jordan. Its regional center was Damascus.)

Compared to the Arab lands surrounding her, Israel is tiny—approximately one tenth of one percent of the land mass in the Middle East, the rest of which is controlled by Arabs. As of May 2006, the estimated population for the entire nation of Israel was only 7,026,000[135]—less than that of New York City.

In all the commotion over Israel versus the Palestinians, people forget that the Arabs already have a Palestinian state—that would be Jordan—that has already been carved out of the original mandate for Palestine. It was from Jordan that Israel captured the West Bank, part of the so-called "occupied Arab territories," but you never hear the "Palestinians" asking Israel to return the West Bank to Jordan. Nor do they suggest that Israel return the Sinai Peninsula to Egypt. (Other "occupied Arab territories" captured in the Six Day War include the Sinai Peninsula and the Gaza Strip, both captured from Egypt, and the Golan Heights region, captured from Syria.)

Does Israel have a right to exist? Of course it does. Jews have had a continuous presence in their homeland for thousands of years. They have had to take every inch of land they now possess in wars they did not start and in which they were outnumbered. The Arabs have ended up with a far greater percentage of "Palestine" than they have.

While Iranian President Mahmoud Ahmadinejad may want to wipe Israel off the map, Western leaders feel otherwise. Speaking at the American Jewish Committee annual meeting, German Chancellor Angela Merkel said, "The right of existence of the state of Israel must never be questioned." At the same event, *Deutsche Welle* reported that "Bush said that the United States has an 'unshakeable' commitment to defend Israel and pledged that his administration would have no contact with the militant Palestinian group Hamas so long as it refuses to recognize the Jewish state."[136]

Kofi Annan, former Secretary-General of the United Nations, said, "Israel has a right, enshrined in numerous United Nations resolutions, to exist in safety within internationally recognised borders."[137]

Does Israel have a right to exist? The UN says it does. Far more importantly, *God* says it does. I would like to close this chapter by quoting Abba Eban, a former Israeli diplomat and politician, on Israel's right to exist. As originally reported in *The New York Times* on November 18, 1981, Eban said:

> Nobody does Israel any service by proclaiming its 'right to exist.'
>
> Israel's right to exist, like that of the United States, Saudi Arabia and 152 other states, is axiomatic and unreserved. Israel's legitimacy is not suspended in midair awaiting acknowledgement....
>
> There is certainly no other state, big or small, young or old, that would consider mere recognition of its 'right to exist' a favor, or a negotiable concession.[138]

# CHAPTER 11

# MUSLIM LANDS IN BIBLE PROPHECY

## Who Is a Muslim? What Is an Arab?

Ethnically, everybody knows who the Jews are: they are, for the most part, the descendents of Abraham through his son Isaac. But Abraham had seven other sons: his firstborn son Ishmael, whose mother was Hagar, and an additional six sons by Keturah, the concubine Abraham married after the death of Sarah. Ishmael had twelve sons: Nebaioth, Kedar, Adbeel, Mibsam, Mishma, Dumah, Massa, Hadad, Tema, Jetur, Naphish, and Kedemah. Keturah's sons were Zimran, Jokshan, Medan, Midian, Ishbak, and Shuah.

After Isaac was born, Abraham sent Hagar and Ishmael away; before he died, Abraham also sent the sons of Keturah away towards the land of the Ishmaelites. There, in what is now known as the Arabian Peninsula, the clans intermingled and intermarried. Their descendents, together with Lot's descendents (the Moabites and the Ammonites) are usually known as Arabs. Thus we can say that most Arabs are in some way related to Abraham. (Lot was

Abraham's nephew.)

Most (but not all) Arabs are Muslims, but not all Muslims are Arabs. To their credit, Muslims do not officially practice racial discrimination: anyone can become a Muslim. So Biblical prophecies don't refer to Muslims, but to Arabs—to the descendents of Abraham through Ishmael.

## The Ishmaelites

Abraham loved his firstborn son Ishmael, and because he interceded for Ishmael, God blessed Ishmael as well as Isaac.

> And God said unto Abraham, As for Sarai thy wife, thou shalt not call her name Sarai, but Sarah *shall* her name *be*. And I will bless her, and give thee a son also of her: yea, I will bless her, and she shall be *a mother* of nations; kings of people shall be of her. Then Abraham fell upon his face, and laughed, and said in his heart, Shall *a child* be born unto him that is an hundred years old? and shall Sarah, that is ninety years old, bear? And Abraham said unto God, O that Ishmael might live before thee! And God said, Sarah thy wife shall bear thee a son indeed; and thou shalt call his name Isaac: and I will establish my covenant with him for an everlasting covenant, *and* with his seed after him. And as for Ishmael, I have heard thee: Behold, I have blessed him, and will make him fruitful, and will multiply him exceedingly; twelve princes shall he beget, and I will make him a great nation. But my covenant will I establish with Isaac, which Sarah shall bear unto thee at this set time in the next year. And he left off talking with him, and God went up from Abraham.
>
> Genesis 17:15 - 22 (KJV)

The Bible tells us that Ishmael did have twelve sons, and that each of those sons became the leader of a nation. At one point in time, when Hagar became pregnant and Sarah was still unable to conceive, "her mistress was despised in her eyes." In retaliation, Sarah treated Hagar harshly, and Hagar ran away. An angel of the Lord appeared to Hagar, told her to return to Sarah, and gave her the following promise:

> And the angel of the LORD said unto her, I will multiply thy seed exceedingly, that it shall not be numbered for multitude. And the angel of the LORD said unto her, Behold, thou *art* with child, and shalt bear a son, and shalt call his name Ishmael; because the LORD hath heard thy affliction. And he will be a wild man; his hand *will be* against every man, and every man's hand against him; and he shall dwell in the presence of all his brethren.
>
> Genesis 16:10 - 12 (KJV)

We see these characteristics in the Arab nations today: Arab hands are lifted, not only against Israel and the West, but against each other, and they dwell in the presence of all their brethren.

## Psalm 83

Psalm 83 foretells a time when Israel's Arab neighbors will gather together against her to cut her off from being a nation:

> [1] Keep not thou silence, O God: hold not thy peace, and be not still, O God.
>
> [2] For, lo, thine enemies make a tumult: and they that hate thee have lifted up the head.
>
> [3] They have taken crafty counsel against thy people, and consulted against thy hidden ones.
>
> [4] They have said, Come, and let us cut them off from *being* a nation; that the name of Israel may be no more in remembrance.
>
> [5] For they have consulted together with one consent:

they are confederate against thee:

⁶ The tabernacles of Edom, and the Ishmaelites; of Moab, and the Hagarenes;

⁷ Gebal, and Ammon, and Amalek; the Philistines with the inhabitants of Tyre;

⁸ Assur also is joined with them: they have holpen the children of Lot.

*Selah*

⁹ Do unto them as *unto* the Midianites; as *to* Sisera, as *to* Jabin, at the brook of Kison:

¹⁰ *Which* perished at Endor: they became *as* dung for the earth.

¹¹ Make their nobles like Oreb, and like Zeeb: yea, all their princes as Zebah, and as Zalmunna:

¹² Who said, Let us take to ourselves the houses of God in possession.

¹³ O my God, make them like a wheel; as the stubble before the wind.

¹⁴ As the fire burneth a wood, and as the flame setteth the mountains on fire;

¹⁵ So persecute them with thy tempest, and make them afraid with thy storm.

¹⁶ Fill their faces with shame; that they may seek thy name, O LORD.

¹⁷ Let them be confounded and troubled for ever; yea, let them be put to shame, and perish:

¹⁸ That *men* may know that thou, whose name alone *is* JEHOVAH, *art* the most high over all the earth.

On May 15, the day after the creation of the State of Israel, the armies of Egypt, Syria, Jordan (then known as Transjordan),

Iraq, Saudi Arabia, and Lebanon invaded the newly proclaimed Jewish state. This was a fulfillment of the first part of this Psalm, which predicted that Israel would be attacked by a confederation consisting of southern Jordan and Saudi Arabia (Edom and the Ishmaelites), central Jordan (Moab and Ammon), Egypt and Saudi Arabia (the Hagarenes[139]), southern Jordan (Gebal), the Sinai desert (Amalek), the Gaza strip (Philistia) southern Lebanon (Tyre), Syria and Iraq (Assur), and the children of Lot (another reference to central Jordan).

The interesting thing about Bible prophecy, however, is that it can be fulfilled more than once. For example, there is a prophecy in Malachi 4:5-6 that was fulfilled once by John the Baptist and will be fulfilled again just before the Second Coming: "Behold, I will send you Elijah the prophet before the coming of the great and dreadful day of the LORD: And he shall turn the heart of the fathers to the children, and the heart of the children to their fathers, lest I come and smite the earth with a curse."

Speaking of John the Baptist, Jesus said, "And if ye will receive it, this is Elias, which was for to come" (Matthew 11:14); however, after the death of John the Baptist and speaking in the future tense, Jesus told His disciples, "Elias verily cometh first, and restoreth all things" (Mark 9:11-12).

So although the Arab nations mentioned in Psalm 83 have already come against Israel in one fulfillment of this prophecy, it appears that this psalm has yet to see its final fulfillment, when they will finally be made "as the stubble before the wind."

In March 2006, Hamas deputy political leader Moussa Abu Marzouk told Reuters that "We believe that Israel has no right to exist." According to Reuters:

> The Hamas charter calls for the destruction of the Jewish state. Both the United States and the European Union have branded Hamas a terrorist organization. But it is popular among Palestinians for charitable works and has a reputation for freedom from corruption.

Hamas deputy political leader Moussa Abu Marzouk told Reuters in an interview that recognizing Israel would negate all Palestinian rights.

"It means a negation of the Palestinian people and their rights and their property, of Jerusalem and the holy sites, as well as negation of their right of return. Therefore the recognition of Israel is not on the agenda," Abu Marzouk said.

"We believe that Israel has no right to exist," he added later in remarks to an Arab audience. "Hamas will never take such a step." [140]

Speaking prophetically, the psalmist said, "They have said, Come, and let us cut them off from *being* a nation; that the name of Israel may be no more in remembrance." Speaking in 2006, Moussa Abu Marzouk said, "We believe that Israel has no right to exist." I believe we can expect to see another fulfillment of Psalm 83 in the very near future.

# CHAPTER 12

# LYING FOR ISLAM

In an earlier chapter, we mentioned Al-Takeyya, the Islamic principle of lying for the sake of Allah.

In "Lying in Islam," Abdullah Al Araby quotes a famous Islamic scholar named al-Ghazali, who wrote:

> One of Mohammed's daughters, Umm Kalthoum, testified that she had never heard the Apostle of Allah condone lying, except in these three situations:
>
> 1. For reconciliation among people.
>
> 2. In war.
>
> 3. Amongst spouses, to keep peace in the family.[141]

Unfortunately, we need to remember that America—along with every country that isn't under Muslim control—is part of what Muslims refer to as *Dar-al-Harb*, the domain or abode of war. We may or not be at war with the Muslims, but—because we aren't Muslims—the Muslims are at war with us. However, because of Al-Takeyya, Muslims don't have to admit their enmity and can instead pretend to be our friends.

It is important to realize that Al-Takeyya, lying for the sake of Allah, pertains to religion just as much as it does to politics. In other words, what Muslim activists say in order to spread Islam may not, in fact, be true.

In the Quran, Mohammed seems to have gone from relatively tolerant to downright violent. It is important to keep in mind that Islamic activists always quote the peaceful, tolerant verses from Mohammed's early ministry even though they are fully aware that most of these passages were superseded by later passages written after he migrated to Medina. The later verses endorse prejudice, intolerance, and terrorism where unbelievers are concerned.

I have heard stories of Muslims who were converted to Islam by people who quoted the peaceful, tolerant parts of the Quran and discussed the more violent verses only after the convert had become a Muslim. By then, the converts were stuck. In Muslim countries, renouncing Islam carries the death penalty.

## The God of the Koran Is Not the God of the Bible

Believe it or not, as much as Islam hates the Christians and the Jews, they actually give Christians and Jews a special, "preferred" status over other infidels. For example, the Soviet Union, which was officially atheist, was seen as being much worse than the US, which was perceived as being Christian. In Islamic law, Jews and Christians are referred to as "people of the Book."

While some lies told by Muslims are told for the sake of Islam, other lies may be perpetrated by Muslims who are ignorant of the truth. Muslim activists in the West have been using the name "God" in place of "Allah" in many translations of the Quran in order to gain legitimacy and acceptance among people with a Judeo-Christian heritage. It may be that many Muslims themselves believe that Allah (as revealed in the Koran) is the same as the Judeo-Christian God revealed in the Bible.

No matter what label you put on him, however, the god of Muhammad is *not* the God of the Bible. The Middle Eastern moon-god was called al-ilah, i.e. *the* god, which was then shortened to Allah in pre-Islamic times. Today, Arab Christians and Arabic-speaking Jews use the word Allah to refer to the God of the Bible, as do Roman Catholics in Malta, Christians in Indonesia, and Christians in the Middle East. However, the "Allah" Who is worshipped by these Christians and Jews is not the same "Allah" who was worshipped by Muhammad and therefore by the Muslims. The Allah worshipped by the Muslims is their original moon-god, Allah. Muhammad was raised as a moon worshipper. But while other pagan Arabs believed that Allah, the moon-god, was the greatest of all gods and the supreme deity in a pantheon of deities, Muhammad decided that Allah was not only the greatest god in a pantheon of many gods, but that Allah was also the *only* god. However, Muhammad never changed Allah's identity. The Allah Muhammad worshipped was the same moon-god Allah his ancestors had worshipped. Muhammad didn't *switch* gods—he just threw away a lot of *extra* gods.

To look at it from another angle, think about this: pagan Arabs worshipped the moon-god Allah by praying toward Mecca several times a day; making a pilgrimage to Mecca; running around the temple of the moon-god called the Kabah; kissing the black stone; killing an animal in sacrifice to the moon-god; throwing stones at the devil; fasting for the month which begins and ends with the crescent moon; etc. All of these are now traditional Muslim practices. In fact, the crescent moon is now seen on the flags of many Muslim nations. Why is that? I submit to you that it is a symbol of the god they worship, and not of my God, the God of the Bible. My God *created* the moon—it says so in Genesis.

# CHAPTER 13

# RUSSIA WILL RISE AGAIN

The Soviet Union may have fallen, but even when things looked their worst for the Russian nation, Bible scholars have historically believed that Russia was destined to play a major role—a superpower role—in the Middle East. And Russia is, in fact, re-establishing itself as a superpower, relying not (for the moment) on its power as a nuclear nation, but on its vast reserves of energy.

According to BBC News, "Energy will bring Russia considerable political power. The world is waiting to see how that power is going to be used."[142]

Russia has more than a fifth of the world's known natural gas reserves and about seven percent of the world's oil. Western Europe already gets a quarter of its gas from Russia.[143]

A control freak among nations, Russia has already used its energy clout to put political pressure on its former satellites. "Rather than a reliable partner, they've found Moscow deeply vindictive toward any neighbor that crosses its interests."[144] *Newsweek International* puts it this way:

Ever since the pro-Western Rose Revolution of November 2003, Georgian leaders say, Moscow's been trying to ruin the country's economy—first by raising gas prices, and in recent months by blocking imports of fruits, vegetables, wine and mineral water. Ditto for Ukraine, hit with a doubling of gas prices, a gas stoppage and a blockade of meat and produce in the wake of its own Orange Revolution. Even poor Moldova, which hasn't had a revolution of any color yet, was hit with a gas hike and a ban on wine exports to Russia after it struck a deal with the European Union sealing the borders of the tiny, Russian-speaking enclave of Transdniestr, which Moscow regards as a protectorate. "Russia treats us like it treated Hungary, Czechoslovakia and Germany in the '50s and '60s," Georgian president Mikhail Saakashvili tells NEWSWEEK. "We are being punished for our attempts to be free."[145]

Western news media are beginning to become aware that Russia could use energy to gain the upper hand over Western nations if we allow it. According to this *Washington Post* editorial:

Western countries should absorb an important lesson. Without a prosperous or technologically advanced economy and with greatly reduced military strength, Mr. Putin hopes to restore Russia's world-power status through its control of gas. That inevitably means manipulating supplies to other countries for political ends. Western countries that do not wish to receive Mr. Putin's ultimatums -- from Germany, France and Britain to the United States, which is being pressed by Russia to line up as a major customer for new Arctic gas fields -- should realize that dependence on Russian gas is not consistent with "energy security." ... Russia cannot be allowed to hold its neighbors, or the world, hostage during a future cold winter.[146]

As reported by the *Los Angeles Times*, Vice President Cheney "accused the government of Vladimir V. Putin of rolling back human rights and using the country's oil and gas reserves as 'tools of intimidation or blackmail.'"[147]

## How Russia Will Affect the Middle East

We know from the book of Ezekiel that Russia will be a major player in Middle Eastern affairs, the leader of a group of Muslim nations that will attack the nation of Israel. From Bible prophecy, we can even pinpoint the time that this will happen: it will be after the re-establishment of the nation of Israel, and it will come at a point in history when Israel "dwelleth safely" (Ezekiel 38:14).

Let's see who the players will be:

> The word of the LORD came to me: Mortal, set your face toward Gog, of the land of Magog, the chief prince of Meshech and Tubal. Prophesy against him and say: Thus says the Lord GOD: I am against you, O Gog, chief prince of Meshech and Tubal; I will turn you around and put hooks into your jaws, and I will lead you out with all your army, horses and horsemen, all of them clothed in full armor, a great company, all of them with shield and buckler, wielding swords. Persia, Ethiopia, and Put are with them, all of them with buckler and helmet; Gomer and all its troops; Beth-togarmah from the remotest parts of the north with all its troops—many peoples are with you.
>
> Ezekiel 38:1-6 (NRSV)

In this prophecy, Gog is a man who comes from the land of Magog and is the chief prince of Meshech and Tubal. Josephus identifies Meshech with the Scythians, an area in Eurasia inhabited by a group of Iranian nomads. Because they were nomads, the location and extent of Scythia varied, so the countries referred to by Magog could include the Caucasus area, including Azerbaijan and Georgia; the Central Asian steppes (Uzbekistan, Turkmenistan,

Tajikistan, Afghanistan); the Altay Mountains area where Mongolia, China, Russia, and Kazakhstan meet; Pakistan and North-Western India, the southern Ukraine, lower Danube river area, and Bulgaria.

Although it's too early to tell how the Gog/Magog war will actually unfold, I think it's very interesting that in 2005 Russia and Iran signed an agreement for Moscow to supply fuel to Iran's new nuclear reactor in Bushehr. In June 2006 Russia and Iran proposed setting up an "energy club" with China and four central Asian states to strengthen regional cooperation and development.[148]

Another interesting tidbit is that MosNews reported in February 2006 that Russian and Turkish naval ships would engage in joint military exercises to be held in the Black Sea.[149] Just a few years ago, it would have been unthinkable for a NATO member to hold joint military exercises with Russia. Look how quickly things are changing in order to line up with the Bible!

When the Soviet Union dissolved, Russia may have looked like it was down and out, but I believe it's in the middle of a resurrection. If Russia is Gog, we can only expect it to grow stronger and stronger as the Gog/Magog war draws near.

# CHAPTER 14

# THE KINGDOM OF ISRAEL

Radical Islam believes that Allah will one day restore the Caliphate, so that the whole world will be under Muslim rule. If the Antichrist rises out of the Muslim nations, this may very well happen—for a brief seven years. But Bible believers know that one day God will restore the kingdom to Israel. Israel will rule the world, and the Messiah—Jesus—will be revealed as her King. In the meanwhile, God's Kingdom still exists in a very real way in the hearts of all believers.

One of the questions Jesus was often asked was this: Are you about to restore the kingdom to Israel? Here's what Jesus told the Pharisees:

> And when he was demanded of the Pharisees, when the kingdom of God should come, he answered them and said, The kingdom of God cometh not with observation: Neither shall they say, Lo here! or, lo there! for, behold, the kingdom of God is within you. And he said unto the disciples, The days will come, when ye shall desire to see one of the days of the Son of man, and ye shall not see it. And they shall

say to you, See here; or, see there: go not after them, nor follow them. For as the lightning, that lighteneth out of the one part under heaven, shineth unto the other part under heaven; so shall also the Son of man be in his day. But first must he suffer many things, and be rejected of this generation. And as it was in the days of Noe [Noah], so shall it be also in the days of the Son of man. They did eat, they drank, they married wives, they were given in marriage, until the day that Noe entered into the ark, and the flood came, and destroyed them all. Likewise also as it was in the days of Lot; they did eat, they drank, they bought, they sold, they planted, they builded; But the same day that Lot went out of Sodom it rained fire and brimstone from heaven, and destroyed them all. Even thus shall it be in the day when the Son of man is revealed. In that day, he which shall be upon the housetop, and his stuff in the house, let him not come down to take it away: and he that is in the field, let him likewise not return back. Remember Lot's wife. Whosoever shall seek to save his life shall lose it; and whosoever shall lose his life shall preserve it. I tell you, in that night there shall be two men in one bed; the one shall be taken, and the other shall be left. Two women shall be grinding together; the one shall be taken, and the other left. Two men shall be in the field; the one shall be taken, and the other left.

Luke 17:20-35

To the Pharisees, Jesus said, you can't *see* the arrival of the Kingdom of God, because the Kingdom of God is within you. Until the Second Coming of Jesus, "the kingdom of God cometh not with observation." There is no earthly government that can claim to be the Kingdom of God, because until His return, "the kingdom of God is within you."

The kingdom of God is in our hearts, and it is a very real

and powerful kingdom even now. But *"in his day,"* as Jesus phrased it, there will be a time when "as the lightning, that lighteneth out of the one part under heaven, shineth unto the other part under heaven; so shall also the Son of man be."

The generation that saw the First Coming of Jesus would not get to see His Second Coming before they died. They would not live to see Him set up His earthly kingdom, with its capital in Jerusalem. The generation that *does* get to see the Second Coming—and I believe it will be this present generation—will see Jesus come suddenly and publicly—like a lightening flash—to the entire, unsuspecting world.

Jesus said, "Watch therefore: for ye know not what hour your Lord doth come. But know this, that if the goodman of the house had known in what watch the thief would come, he would have watched, and would not have suffered his house to be broken up. Therefore be ye also ready: for in such an hour as ye think not the Son of man cometh" (Matthew 24:42-44).

Jesus' disciples were so eager to know when Jesus would restore the Kingdom of God that it was the last thing they asked Him about before He ascended into heaven:

> When they therefore were come together, they asked of him, saying, Lord, wilt thou at this time restore again the kingdom to Israel? And he said unto them, It is not for you to know the times or the seasons, which the Father hath put in his own power. But ye shall receive power, after that the Holy Ghost is come upon you: and ye shall be witnesses unto me both in Jerusalem, and in all Judaea, and in Samaria, and unto the uttermost part of the earth. And when he had spoken these things, while they beheld, he was taken up; and a cloud received him out of their sight. And while they looked stedfastly toward heaven as he went up, behold, two men stood by them in white apparel; Which also said, Ye men of Galilee, why stand ye gazing up into heaven? this same Jesus, which is taken up from you into heaven,

shall so come in like manner as ye have seen him go into heaven.

Acts 1:6-11

When Jesus comes in the clouds, those of us who are believers will be caught up to be with Him:

> For this we say unto you by the word of the Lord, that we which are alive and remain unto the coming of the Lord shall not prevent them which are asleep. For the Lord himself shall descend from heaven with a shout, with the voice of the archangel, and with the trump of God: and the dead in Christ shall rise first: Then we which are alive and remain shall be caught up together with them in the clouds, to meet the Lord in the air: and so shall we ever be with the Lord.

1 Thessalonians 4:16-17

There is a generation that will see Jesus coming like a flash of lightening—coming in the clouds. Coming suddenly, for those who are ready. Coming with all who are in Christ. Coming, not in mercy, but in judgment. "And Enoch also, the seventh from Adam, prophesied of these, saying, Behold, the Lord cometh with ten thousands of his saints, To execute judgment upon all..." (Jude 1:14-15)

The kingdom of heaven starts small and grows large. Jesus said, "The kingdom of heaven is like to a grain of mustard seed, which a man took, and sowed in his field: Which indeed is the least of all seeds: but when it is grown, it is the greatest among herbs, and becometh a tree, so that the birds of the air come and lodge in the branches thereof." (Matthew 13:31-32).

This Bible tells us that King Nebuchadnezzar had a dream that was interpreted by the prophet Daniel (see Daniel, Chapter 2). In this dream, God showed Nebuchadnezzar a statue with a head of gold, chest and arms of silver, belly and thighs of brass, legs of iron, and feet of iron mixed with clay. "Thou sawest," Daniel told the king, "till that a stone was cut out without hands, which smote the image upon his feet that were of iron and clay, and brake them to pieces. Then was the iron, the clay, the brass, the silver, and the gold, broken to pieces together, and became like the chaff of the summer threshingfloors; and the wind carried them away, that no place was found for them: and the stone that smote the image became a great mountain, and filled the whole earth (verses 31-35).

The fourth kingdom (the legs of iron) was the Roman Empire. According to Matthew Henry:

> ...it is the Roman monarchy that is here intended, because it was in the time of that monarchy, and when it was at its height, that the kingdom of Christ was set up in the world by the preaching of the everlasting gospel. The Roman kingdom was strong as iron (v. 40), witness the prevalency of that kingdom against all that contended with it for many ages. That kingdom broke in pieces the Grecian empire and afterwards quite destroyed the nation of the Jews. Towards the latter end of the Roman monarchy it grew very weak, and branched into ten kingdoms, which were as the toes of these feet. Some of these were weak as clay, others strong as iron, v. 42. Endeavours were used to unite and cement them for the strengthening of the empire, but in vain:[150]

It should be mentioned here that Bible scholars disagree about whether the feet of iron and clay are part of the original Roman kingdom (the legs of iron) or whether they are a fifth kingdom—the end-times kingdom of the Antichrist. Because Bible prophecies can be fulfilled more than one time, I see no reason why "the feet kingdom" can't represent both. We do know for certain, however, that the kingdom of the Lord Jesus Christ was initiated during the time of the Roman Empire.

In Nebuchadnezzar's dream, "...a stone was cut out without

hands, which smote the image upon his feet *that were* of iron and clay, and brake them to pieces. [35] Then was the iron, the clay, the brass, the silver, and the gold, broken to pieces together, and became like the chaff of the summer threshingfloors; and the wind carried them away, that no place was found for them: and the stone that smote the image became a great mountain, and filled the whole earth." (Daniel 34-36).

"And in the days of these kings shall the God of heaven set up a kingdom, which shall never be destroyed: and the kingdom shall not be left to other people, *but* it shall break in pieces and consume all these kingdoms, and it shall stand for ever." (Daniel 2:44).

Speaking of Himself, Jesus said, "What is this then that is written, The stone which the builders rejected, the same is become the head of the corner? Whosoever shall fall upon that stone shall be broken; but on whomsoever it shall fall, it will grind him to powder" (Luke 20:17-18).

The Kingdom of Heaven was initiated during the First Coming of the Lord Jesus Christ; it will be completely fulfilled at the Second Coming, when all earthly kingdoms are done away with. In those days, God will "restore again the kingdom to Israel," and Jesus Christ will be her King. "At that time they shall call Jerusalem the throne of the LORD; and all the nations shall be gathered unto it, to the name of the LORD, to Jerusalem: neither shall they walk any more after the imagination of their evil heart" (Jeremiah 3:17).

Zechariah 14 foretells a battle that will take place in Jerusalem. This will be in the very last of the last days, after the event the Church calls the Rapture, when "… the Lord himself shall descend from heaven with a shout, with the voice of the archangel, and with the trump of God: and the dead in Christ shall rise first: Then we which are alive *and* remain shall be caught up together with them in the clouds, to meet the Lord in the air: and so shall we ever be with the Lord" (1 Thessalonians 4:16-17).

At this last battle for Jerusalem, Israel will be even more

vastly outnumbered than usual, and it will look at first as though she is losing the battle:

> Behold, the day of the LORD cometh, and thy spoil shall be divided in the midst of thee. For I will gather all nations against Jerusalem to battle; and the city shall be taken, and the houses rifled, and the women ravished; and half of the city shall go forth into captivity, and the residue of the people shall not be cut off from the city.
>
> Zechariah 14:1-2

According to Zechariah, God will gather all nations against Jerusalem. In her own strength, Israel will be unable to defend herself against the world's armies, and she will appear to be losing badly. Zechariah doesn't tell us how long the battle will take, but it looks as though the battle will go on for some time—time enough for the city to be taken and looted, the women ravished, and half of the people to go into captivity. Before the other half of the people are taken, however, God will intervene in a supernatural way:

> Then shall the LORD go forth, and fight against those nations, as when he fought in the day of battle. And his feet shall stand in that day upon the mount of Olives, which *is* before Jerusalem on the east, and the mount of Olives shall cleave in the midst thereof toward the east and toward the west, *and there shall be* a very great valley; and half of the mountain shall remove toward the north, and half of it toward the south. And ye shall flee *to* the valley of the mountains; for the valley of the mountains shall reach unto Azal: yea, ye shall flee, like as ye fled from before the earthquake in the days of Uzziah king of Judah: and the LORD my God shall come, *and* all the saints with thee.

For "all the saints" to be with the Lord, this battle has to take place after all the saints—both living and dead—have been caught up to be with Him. The Bible teaches in many places that the saints will not only accompany the Lord in the Battle for Jerusalem, but will also help him judge the world:

> And Enoch also, the seventh from Adam, prophesied of these, saying, Behold, the Lord cometh with ten thousands of his saints, To execute judgment upon all, and to convince all that are ungodly among them of all their ungodly deeds which they have ungodly committed, and of all their hard *speeches* which ungodly sinners have spoken against him.
>
> Jude 1:14-15

> But the saints of the most High shall take the kingdom, and possess the kingdom for ever, even for ever and ever.
>
> Daniel 7:18

> I beheld, and the same horn made war with the saints, and prevailed against them; Until the Ancient of days came, and judgment was given to the saints of the most High; and the time came that the saints possessed the kingdom.
>
> Da 7:21-22

> Do ye not know that the saints shall judge the world? and if the world shall be judged by you, are ye unworthy to judge the smallest matters?
>
> 1Co 6:2a

Getting back to Zechariah's account of this battle, we are told that the Lord will smite all the people who have fought against Jerusalem with a plague that sounds to modern ears very much like nuclear weapons, but could just as easily be a flesh eating disease of some sort: "And this shall be the plague wherewith the LORD will smite all the people that have fought against Jerusalem; Their flesh shall consume away while they stand upon their feet, and their eyes shall consume away in their holes, and their tongue shall consume away in their mouth" (Zechariah 14:12).

As if this plague weren't enough, the Lord will also turn the enemies of Israel against each other: "And it shall come to pass in that day, *that* a great tumult from the LORD shall be among them; and they shall lay hold every one on the hand of his neighbour, and his hand shall rise up against the hand of his neighbour" (Zechariah 14:13).

Where are the Jews in all of this? They have probably been fighting all along, because Zechariah continues his account of the battle as follows:

> And Judah also shall fight at Jerusalem; and the wealth of all the heathen round about shall be gathered together, gold, and silver, and apparel, in great abundance. And so shall be the plague of the horse, of the mule, of the camel, and of the ass, and of all the beasts that shall be in these tents, as this plague. And it shall come to pass, *that* every one that is left of all the nations which came against Jerusalem shall even go up from year to year to worship the King, the LORD of hosts, and to keep the feast of tabernacles. And it shall be, *that* whoso will not come up of *all* the families of the earth unto Jerusalem to worship the King, the LORD of hosts, even upon them shall be no rain. And if the family of Egypt go not up, and come not, that *have* no *rain*; there shall be the plague, wherewith the LORD will smite the heathen that come not up to keep the feast of tabernacles. This shall be the punishment of Egypt, and the punishment of all nations that come not up to keep the feast of tabernacles.
>
> Zechariah 14:14-19 (KJV)

You may have noticed that I skipped a portion of Zechariah's account that talks mainly about what happens after the battle:

> And it shall come to pass in that day, *that* the light
> shall not be clear, *nor* dark: But it shall be one day
> which shall be known to the LORD, not day, nor
> night: but it shall come to pass, *that* at evening time
> it shall be light. And it shall be in that day, *that*
> living waters shall go out from Jerusalem; half of
> them toward the former sea, and half of them toward
> the hinder sea: in summer and in winter shall it be.
> And the LORD shall be king over all the earth: in
> that day shall there be one LORD, and his name one.
> All the land shall be turned as a plain from Geba to
> Rimmon south of Jerusalem: and it shall be lifted up,
> and inhabited in her place, from Benjamin's gate
> unto the place of the first gate, unto the corner gate,
> and *from* the tower of Hananeel unto the king's
> winepresses. And *men* shall dwell in it, and there
> shall be no more utter destruction; but Jerusalem
> shall be safely inhabited.
>
> Zechariah 14:6-11

Zechariah tells us that "… the LORD shall be king over all the earth: in that day shall there be one LORD, and his name one."

After the Lord wins the battle for Jerusalem, He will rule the world. There will be only one King, and the world will worship only one God. It is at this time that God will "restore the kingdom to Israel," but although Jerusalem will be the capital of the world, "the kingdom" will be God's and what used to be referred to as "nations" are now referred to as "families." After Jesus returns, the world will not longer be organized by nations, but by families, and Jerusalem will—at long last, and after thousands of years—be safely inhabited.

# PART 3—HOW TO PROTECT YOUR FAMILY FROM WEAPONS OF MASS DESTRUCTION AND OTHER DISASTERS

# CHAPTER 15

# THE US CITIES MOST LIKELY TO BE ATTACKED WITH WMDS

Just because you don't live in New York City or Washington, DC or near a military base, don't think you're safe from a terrorist attack.

In 1997 the Nunn-Lugar-Domenici Domestic Preparedness Program began to train first responders in 120 cities deemed most vulnerable to WMDs. Later, these 120 cities were expanded and amended to a list of 157 cities and counties. A map of these Domestic Preparedness Programs can be found at http://cns.miis.edu/research/cbw/120city.htm.

From what I've read, many factors went into deciding what might constitute a terrorist target, some of which included population density, proximity to nuclear plants or waste sites or to a landmark-cultural-heritage center, importance as a shipping or trucking route or port, communications hub or other critical infrastructure site.

If you live in what appears to be a targeted area, and you are in a position to do so, one of the most important things you can do to protect your family is to move. Move to a place that is of little or no interest to terrorists. This won't absolutely guarantee your safety, but it will certainly improve your statistical chances.

Here is a list of the original 120 cities:[151]

## 120 US Cities on the Domestic Preparedness List

| | |
|---|---|
| Akron, Ohio | Des Moines, Iowa |
| Albuquerque, N.M. | Detroit, Mich. |
| Amarillo, Texas | El Paso, Texas |
| Anaheim, Calif. | Fort Wayne, Ind. |
| Anchorage, Alaska | Fort Worth, Texas |
| Arlington, Texas | Freemont, Calif. |
| Arlington, Va. | Fresno, Calif. |
| Atlanta, Ga. | Ft. Lauderdale, Fla. |
| Aurora, Colo. | Garland, Texas |
| Austin, Texas | Glendale, Ariz. |
| Bakersfield, Calif. | Glendale, Calif. |
| Baltimore, Md. | Grand Rapids, Mich. |
| Baton Rouge, La. | Greensboro, N.C. |
| Birmingham, Ala. | Hialeah, Fla. |
| Boston, Mass. | Honolulu, Hawaii |
| Buffalo, N.Y. | Houston, Texas |
| Charlotte, N.C. | Huntington Beach, Calif. |
| Chattanooga, Tenn. | Huntsville, Ala. |
| Chesapeake, Va. | Indianapolis, Ind. |
| Chicago, Ill. | Irving, Texas |
| Cincinnati, Ohio | Jackson, Miss. |
| Cleveland, Ohio | Jacksonville, Fla. |
| Colorado Springs, Colo. | Jersey City, N.J. |
| Columbus, Ga. | Kansas City, Kan. |
| Columbus, Ohio | Kansas City, Mo. |
| Corpus Christi, Texas | Knoxville, Tenn. |
| Dallas, Texas | Las Vegas, Nev. |
| Dayton, Ohio | Lexington-Fayette, Ky. |
| Denver, Colo. | Lincoln, Neb. |

Little Rock, Ark.
Long Beach, Calif.
Los Angeles, Calif.
Louisville, Ky.
Lubbock, Texas
Madison, Wis.
Memphis, Tenn.
Mesa, Ariz.
Metairie, La.
Miami, Fla.
Milwaukee, Wis.
Minneapolis, Minn.
Mobile, Ala.
Modesto, Calif.
Montgomery, Ala.
Nashville, Tenn.
New Orleans, La.
New York, N.Y.
Newark, N.J.
Newport News, Va.
Norfolk, Va.
Oakland, Calif.
Oklahoma City, Okla.
Omaha, Neb.
Orlando, Fla.
Philadelphia, Pa.
Phoenix, Ariz.
Pittsburgh, Pa.
Portland, Ore.
Providence, R.I.
Raleigh, N.C.

Richmond, Va.
Riverside, Calif.
Rochester, N.Y.
Sacramento, Calif.
Salt Lake City, Utah
San Antonio, Texas
San Bernardino, Calif.
San Diego, Calif.
San Francisco, Calif.
San Jose, Calif.
Santa Ana, Calif.
Seattle, Wash.
Shreveport, La.
Spokane, Wash.
Springfield, Mass.
St. Louis, Mo.
St. Paul, Minn.
St. Petersburg, Fla.
Stockton, Calif.
Syracuse, N.Y.
Tacoma, Wash.
Tampa, Fla.
Toledo, Ohio
Tucson, Ariz.
Tulsa, Okla.
Virginia Beach, Va.
Warren, Mich.
Washington, D.C.
Wichita, Kan.
Worcester, Mass.
Yonkers, N.Y.

## Don't Live There?  You Still Aren't Safe!

Unfortunately, just because your city or county isn't listed as one of the top terrorist targets, you can't assume you're safe from terrorist attack. I hate to tell you this, but actually *nobody* is safe. This is because one goal of terrorists is to terrorize. They want to ensure that nobody feels safe. How can they do this? One way is by striking where they aren't expected. This is why everybody needs to be prepared for terrorist attacks. However, while moving to a low-risk area won't make you immune to terrorists, it will increase your statistical chances of avoiding a terrorist attack.

## Location, Location, Location

As we saw with Hurricanes Katrina and Rita, a terrorist attack isn't necessarily the only disaster it would be wise to prepare for. The FEMA website (www.fema.gov) has a wealth of disaster preparedness information on terrorism, but also on topics including household chemicals, dam failure, earthquake, fire, flood, hazardous material, heat, hurricane, landslides, nuclear incidents, thunderstorms, tornados, tsunamis, volcanoes, wildfires and winter storms. Most of these topics also have links to maps or tables showing what your risk would be for that particular kind of disaster if you live in a particular location. For example, the earthquake topic contains a link entitled "What is the earthquake risk where I live?" Clicking on the link takes you to a table entitled "Earthquake Risk by State and Territory." The section on dam failure tells you how to find out whether a particular dam has a high-hazard or significant-hazard potential.

If you are thinking about moving from a high-terror-risk location, it would be a good idea to research your possible new location from a disaster preparedness point of view. You wouldn't want to move to some peaceful rural neighborhood in order to avoid a terrorist attack only to find that you'd just moved downstream from a high-hazard dam or right in the middle of tornado alley.

# CHAPTER 16

# ISLAMIST WEAPONS OF MASS DESTRUCTION

According to the Monterey Institute's Center for Nonproliferation Studies, "The most widely used definition of 'weapons of mass destruction' in official US documents is *'nuclear, chemical, and biological weapons.'*"[152]

In a statement issued on September 17, 2002, President Bush said, "The gravest danger our Nation faces lies at the crossroads of radicalism and technology. Our enemies have openly declared that they are seeking weapons of mass destruction, and evidence indicates that they are doing so with determination. The United States will not allow these efforts to succeed. ...History will judge harshly those who saw this coming danger but failed to act. In the new world we have entered, the only path to peace and security is the path of action."[153]

President Bush went on to say: "Weapons of mass destruction could enable adversaries to inflict massive harm on the United States, our military forces at home and abroad, and our friends and allies. Some states, including several that have supported and continue to support terrorism, already possess WMD and are seeking even greater capabilities, as tools of coercion and intimidation. For them, these are not weapons of last resort, but militarily useful weapons of choice intended to overcome our nation's advantages in conventional forces and to deter us from responding to aggression against our friends and allies in regions of vital interest. In addition, terrorist groups are seeking to acquire WMD with the stated purpose of killing large numbers of our people and those of friends and allies—without compunction and without warning."[154]

## Countries with WMD Capabilities

Weapons of mass destruction—especially WMDs that can be used by terrorists—are of grave concern to every thinking person. Today, many nations possess WMD capabilities—among them many Muslim nations. Details of who has what—and where they may have hidden it—are notoriously hard to come by. Most weapons of mass destruction programs cannot be independently verified because of the secrecy with which they are implemented.

Let's be clear on this: it isn't *only* Muslim nations that possess WMDs. We are concerned about Muslim WMD capabilities because we are concerned about Muslim terrorist WMD capabilities. But as you can see from the chart below, various WMD programs exist in many nations. Please note that this chart summarizes data available from many public sources and may not be complete or accurate.

| Country | Nuclear | Chemical | Biological |
|---------|---------|----------|------------|
| Algeria | X | X | ? |
| Belarus | X | | |
| Brazil | ? | | |
| Bulgaria | | | X |
| Chile | | X | |
| China | X | X | X |
| Cuba | | | X |

| Country | Nuclear | Chemical | Biological |
|---|---|---|---|
| Ethiopia | | X | |
| Egypt | | X | X |
| France | X | X | |
| India | X | X | X |
| Indonesia | | X | |
| Iran | X | X | X |
| Iraq | X | X | X |
| Israel | X | X | X |
| Kazakhstan | X | | |
| Laos | | X | X |
| Libya | | X | X |
| Myanmar | | X | |
| North Korea | X | X | X |
| Pakistan | X | X | X |
| Romania | | | X |
| Russia | X | X | X |
| Saudi Arabia | ? | | ? |
| Serbia | X | X | |
| South Africa | X | X | X |
| South Korea | | X | X |
| Sudan | | X | ? |
| Syria | | X | X |
| Taiwan | | X | X |
| Thailand | | X | |
| Ukraine | X | | |
| Vietnam | | X | X |
| UK | X | X | |
| US | X | X | X |
| Yemen | | | ? |

? = Unconfirmed; X = has or has had some form of WMD program in this area

## Suicide Bombers with WMDs

WMDs are particularly disturbing when you think about the possibility that they might be carried by a suicide bomber. Whether it's a pathogen-laden biological aerosol, a canister filled with chemical gas, or a nuclear suitcase bomb, modern WMD capabilities make it possible for a single person to unleash mass destruction upon an innocent and unsuspecting populace. This chapter discusses a number of WMD *possibilities*—things that have been made possible by modern weapons technologies. Categories discussed are biological, chemical, and nuclear/dirty bomb WMDs.

## Biological WMDs

There are three broad categories of biological WMDs: *viruses* such as smallpox and encephalitis; *bacteria* such as anthrax and plague; and *toxins* like botulinum and ricin. To terrorists, the advantages of using bioweapons would be the fact that they are not easily traced or detected; that viruses and bacteria can multiply on their own; and that very small quantities can have a significant impact. The effect of most biological weapons is not immediate—it takes time to "come down" with an illness. This could be either a benefit or a drawback, depending on the terrorist's point of view. Biological weapons are also difficult to obtain and produce, which would be a definite downside.

Bioterrorism agents are typically found in nature, but before they can be used as weapons, they must usually be modified in order to increase their ability to cause disease, make them drug resistant, or to increase their viability or their ability to spread. Depending on the agent, biological WMDs can be spread through air, through water, through food, or through person-to-person contact.

## Nuclear and Dirty Bombs

Radiological dispersal devices (RDDs) are commonly

known as "dirty bombs" in which radiological material is packed around a core of explosive. When the bomb goes off, it disperses the material over a wide area, possibly causing burns and poisoning in the short term and cancer and groundwater contamination in the long term. The radiological material necessary to make a dirty bomb can be found in research laboratories, hospitals, and industrial facilities—or even, on a very small scale, in home smoke detectors.

In general, nuclear weapons are difficult to manufacture without detection. They are also very expensive to make and difficult to transport. However, while so far as we know, only actual governments possess full-size nuclear bombs, there are some nuclear bombs that are only the size of a small suitcase, which is why they are known as "suitcase bombs." A number of suitcase bombs have been unaccounted for since the fall of the Soviet Union, and this may be the source of the suitcase bombs that Al Qaeda is reported to possess. (See Page 60.)

## Missiles

Missiles are conventional weapons, and while they aren't generally thought of as WMDs, they certainly cause mass destruction when they hit a densely populated target. Normally, we think of missiles as belonging to the military, but terrorists have also been able to obtain them.

The Lebanese terror group Hezbollah has already fired many Katyusha rockets at Israeli targets. Now, the world has learned that Iran has doubled Hezbollah's firing range by supplying them with long-range missiles capable of striking all of Israel's major population centers.[155] In May 2006 Israeli Defense Forces Colonel Gal Hirsch said that "Hezbollah is a wing of the Iranian effort to create a frontline against the West."[156]

# CHAPTER 17
# WHAT TO DO BEFORE DISASTER STRIKES

## 1. Create a Plan

### Before the Attack Occurs

- Do a hazard and risk assessment for yourself and your family.
- Learn the emergency response plans of your family's schools and employers. If an evacuation should be necessary, where would they take their students or employees?
- Prepare a list of emergency names and phone numbers on a small card to be carried by every family member. At a minimum it should include:
    - o Emergency contact name and phone number
    - o Out-of-state contact name & phone number
    - o Neighborhood meeting place & meeting place phone number

- o "Dial 9-1-1 for Emergencies!" (include this to be sure children have this number)
- Find out what plans, procedures, and guidelines are used by the response agencies and organizations in your community. Examples include:
  - o All-hazards emergency operations plan
  - o Incident-specific c annexes**
  - o Volunteer coordination guidelines
  - o Health department staff assignments
  - o Communication plans
  - o Individual/family care plans
  - o Command and management systems and authorities
  - o Continuity of operations plan (COOP)[157]
- Make copies of all your important documents, records and photos and arrange to have them stored by a friend or relative in a geographically distant location. Be sure to include copies of your:
  - o Driver's licenses
  - o Social security cards
  - o Passports (if you have them)
  - o Deeds
  - o Wills
  - o Insurance policies
  - o Prescription information: doctor, medication, dosage, pharmacy name, prescription number
  - o Photos of family members (including pets) for ID purposes
- Make copies of the same information and put it and some cash in a waterproof container.
- Many shelters will not allow pets; others will allow pets only if they are in carriers. Have a plan (and carriers) for your pets.
- Identify a meeting place near home where your family can assemble, plus another away from your neighborhood in case your neighborhood is unreachable.

## 2. Assemble Supplies

You will want three sets of emergency supplies: a large supply for emergencies in which you don't have to evacuate; a 72-hour "go kit" for emergencies in which you do have to evacuate; and smaller kits for each family car in case you aren't at home when the emergency occurs.

In addition to food and bottled water, you will want to include first aid supplies, extra prescription drugs, a hand crank/solar powered radio and flashlights, and a solar cell phone charger.

The Department of Homeland Security has a web site called Ready.gov devoted to disaster preparedness that is well worth visiting. You can find it at http://www.ready.gov/

On its website, the Department of Homeland Security provides a list of recommended supplies, which we have taken the liberty of providing for you as Appendix A. More detailed lists are also provided, under the following categories:

## Water & Food

### Water

- One gallon of water per person per day, for drinking and sanitation.
- Children, nursing mothers, and sick people may need more water.
- If you live in a warm weather climate more water may be necessary.
- Store water tightly in clean plastic containers such as soft drink bottles.
- Keep *at least* a three-day supply of water per person.

### Food

- Store *at least* a three-day supply of non-perishable food.

- Select foods that require no refrigeration, preparation or cooking and little or no water.
- Pack a manual can opener and eating utensils.
- Choose foods your family will eat.
  - Ready-to-eat canned meats, fruits and vegetables
  - Protein or fruit bars
  - Dry cereal or granola
  - Peanut butter
  - Dried fruit
  - Nuts
  - Crackers
  - Canned juices
  - Non-perishable pasteurized milk
  - High energy foods
  - Vitamins
  - Food for infants
  - Comfort/stress foods

Homeland Security also recommends that you download the PDF "Food and Water in an Emergency" from FEMA and the American Red Cross (100k) located at http://www.redcross.org/static/file_cont39_lang0_24.pdf. This publication points out that in time of disaster you might not have access to food, water and electricity for days or even weeks. "Food and Water in an Emergency" is provided as Appendix B.

# CHAPTER 18

# HOW TO PROTECT YOUR FAMILY FROM CHEMICAL WARFARE

*Intelligence reporting indicates that nearly 40 terrorist organizations, insurgencies, or cults have used, possessed, or expressed an interest in chemical, biological, radiological, or nuclear agents or weapons.*
John D. Negroponte, Director of National Intelligence[158]

Chemical warfare uses toxic chemical substances rather than explosives (such as bombs or bullets) or living organisms. (The use of living organisms is considered to be biological warfare.)

Chemical warfare agents take many forms: some contain a cyanide group that prevents the body from using oxygen; some cause large, painful blisters on exposed skin; nerve agents disrupt the neurotransmitters that allow nerves to transmit messages to organs; pulmonary or choking agents disrupt a victim's ability to breathe.

To protect yourself against chemical warfare, you need to cover all exposed skin and have clean air to breathe. Much of the information in this chapter is from Ready.gov, a website published by the US Department of Homeland Security. The Ready.gov information is excellent, as far as it goes. However, we will cover some topics *not* covered by Ready.gov later in this chapter.

# Clean Air[159]

Many potential terrorist attacks could send tiny microscopic "junk" into the air. For example, an explosion may release very fine debris that can cause lung damage. A biological attack may release germs that can make you sick if inhaled or absorbed through open cuts. Many of these agents can only hurt you if they get into your body, so think about **creating a barrier** between yourself and any contamination.

Nose and Mouth Protection

Face masks or dense-weave cotton material, that **snugly covers your nose and mouth** and is specifically fit for each member of the family. Do whatever you can to make the best fit possible for children.

Be prepared to improvise with what you have on hand to protect your nose, mouth, eyes and cuts in your skin. Anything that fits snugly over your nose and mouth, including any dense-weave cotton material, can help filter contaminants in an emergency. It is very important that most of the air you breathe comes through the mask or cloth, not around it. Do whatever you can to make the best fit possible for children. There are also a variety of face masks readily available in hardware stores that are rated based on how small a particle they can filter in an industrial setting.

Given the different types of attacks that could

occur, there is not one solution for masking. For instance, simple cloth face masks can filter some of the airborne "junk" or germs you might breathe into your body, but will probably not protect you from chemical gases. **Still, something over your nose and mouth in an emergency is better than nothing.** Limiting how much "junk" gets into your body may impact whether or not you get sick or develop disease.

### Other Barriers

- **Heavyweight plastic garbage bags** or **plastic sheeting**
- **Duct tape**
- **Scissors**

There are circumstances when staying put and creating a barrier between yourself and potentially contaminated air outside, a process known as **"shelter-in-place,"** is a matter of survival. You can use these things to tape up windows, doors and air vents if you need to seal off a room from outside contamination. Consider precutting and labeling these materials. Anything you can do in advance will save time when it counts.

Use available information to assess the situation. If you see large amounts of debris in the air, or if local authorities say the air is badly contaminated, you can use these things to tape up windows, doors and air vents if you need to seal off a room. Read more: Deciding to Stay or Go [page 164].

## HEPA (High Efficiency Particulate Air Filtration) Filter Fans

Once you have sealed a room with plastic sheeting and duct tape you may have created a better barrier between you and any contaminants that may be outside. However, no seal is perfect and some leakage is likely. In addition to which, you may find yourself in a space that is already contaminated to some degree.

Consider a portable air purifier, with a HEPA filter, to help remove contaminants from the room where you are sheltering. These highly efficient filters have small sieves that can capture very tiny particles, including some biological agents. Once trapped within a HEPA filter contaminants cannot get into your body and make you sick. While these filters are excellent at filtering dander, dust, molds, smoke, biological agents and other contaminants, they will not stop chemical gases.

Some people, particularly those with severe allergies and asthma, use HEPA filters in masks, portable air purifiers as well as in larger home or industrial models to continuously filter the air.

## Gas Masks

For some reason, the Ready.gov website doesn't mention gas masks, which are respirators worn over the nose and mouth—or sometimes the entire face—to protect the wearer from toxic airborne gasses (like the chlorine gas of WWI) or particulates (such as many biologic agents that spread by inhalation). The gas mask removes the toxic material and returns clean air to the wearer.

Gas masks, gas mask filters, and other emergency supplies are readily available over the internet at this point in time. It would be wise to buy enough masks for your family now, because once another terrorist attack occurs on U.S. soil, there will be a run on these items.

It is my opinion, and the opinion of many security experts, that having the right gas mask for every member of your family will be the single most effective piece of equipment you can have, whether you evacuate or shelter in place. Be sure you get an "NBC" (Nuclear-Biological-Chemical) gas mask, and make sure it is newly manufactured—not just "new" as in "never used." Some "new" gas masks sold on the Internet are actually decades old and will only give you a false sense of security. In addition to NBC-rated gas masks for adults, NBC infant wraps and NBC pet protection systems are also available.

## Other Safety Equipment

An NBC-rated protective suit offers body protection against chemical, biological, and nuclear contaminants.

## Deciding to Stay or Go[160]

Depending on your circumstances and the nature of the attack, the first important decision is whether you stay put or get away. You should understand and plan for both possibilities. Use common sense and available information, including what you are learning here, to determine if there is immediate danger.

In any emergency, local authorities may or may not immediately be able to provide information on what is happening and what you should do. However, you should monitor TV or radio news reports for information or official instructions as they become available. If you're specifically told to evacuate or seek medical treatment, do so immediately.

## Staying Put

Whether you are at home, work or elsewhere, there may be situations when it's simply best to stay where you are and avoid any uncertainty outside.

There are other circumstances when staying put and creating a barrier between yourself and potentially contaminated air outside, a process known as "sealing the room," is a matter of survival. Use available information to assess the situation. If you see large amounts of debris in the air, or if local authorities say the air is badly contaminated, you may want to take this kind of action.

The process used to seal the room is considered a temporary protective measure to create a barrier between you and potentially contaminated air outside. It is a type of sheltering in place that requires preplanning.

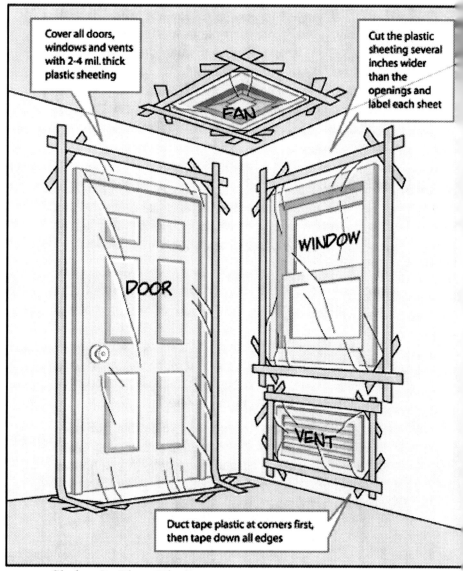

Shelter-In-Place Diagram

## To "Shelter in Place and Seal the Room"

- Bring your family and pets **inside**.

- **Lock** doors, close windows, air vents and fireplace dampers.
- **Turn off** fans, air conditioning and forced air heating systems.
- **Take your emergency supply kit** unless you have reason to believe it has been contaminated.
- **Go into an interior room** with few windows, if possible.
- **Seal** all windows, doors and air vents with plastic sheeting and duct tape. Consider measuring and cutting the sheeting in advance to save time.
- Be prepared to **improvise** and use what you have on hand to **seal gaps** so that you create a barrier between yourself and any contamination.
- Local authorities may not immediately be able to provide information on what is happening and what you should do. However, you should **watch TV, listen to the radio or check the Internet often for official news** and instructions as they become available.

## Getting Away

There may be conditions under which you will decide to get away, or there may be situations when you are ordered to leave. Plan how you will assemble your family and anticipate where you will go. Choose several destinations in different directions so you have options in an emergency.

## Create an evacuation plan:

- **Plan places** where your family will meet, both within and outside of your immediate neighborhood.
- If you have a car, keep a **half tank of gas** in it at all times in case you need to evacuate.
- Become familiar with **alternate routes** and other means of transportation out of your area.
- If you **do not have a car**, plan how you will leave if you have to.

- **Take your emergency supply kit** unless you have reason to believe it has been contaminated.
- **Lock** the door behind you.
- Take your **pets** with you, but understand that only service animals may be permitted in public shelters. Plan how you will care for your pets in an emergency.

If time allows:

- Call or email the "out-of-state" contact in your family communications plan.
- Tell them where you are going.
- If there is damage to your home and you are instructed to do so, shut off water, gas and electricity before leaving.
- Leave a note telling others when you left and where you are going.
- Check with neighbors who may need a ride.

## Learn how and when to turn off utilities:

If there is damage to your home or you are instructed to turn off your utilities:

- Locate the electric, gas and water shut-off valves.
- Keep necessary tools near gas and water shut-off valves.
- Teach family members how to turn off utilities.
- If you turn the gas off, a professional must turn it back on. Do not attempt to do this yourself.

## Plan for your pets:

- **Pets should not be left behind**, but understand that only service animals may be permitted in public shelters. Plan how you will care for your pets in an emergency.
- **Store** extra food, water and supplies for your pet.

# CHAPTER 19

# HOW TO PROTECT YOUR FAMILY FROM BIOLOGICAL WARFARE

Biological weapons can be delivered in several ways. They can be put into food or water supplies, where they would be ingested. They can be aerosolized, or sprayed into the air where they would be inhaled. In some cases, an aerosolized cloud of the agent would be visible, in others not. If—and this is a big if—you are aware of the attack at the time it occurs, you may be able to shelter in place long enough to avoid the worst of the attack. If FEMA is aware of an attack, it can broadcast a warning, along with emergency instructions, on the Emergency Broadcast System.

Treatments for biological agents include antidotes, antibiotics, and pumping of the stomach. For some possible threats, vaccines are available. However, because you can't see germs with the naked eye and symptoms often take time to develop, public health systems may be unable to pinpoint bioterrorism right away. Even after symptoms start developing, they will often mirror ones exhibited by someone with a cold or the flu. There are, however, some things you can do to increase your chances of surviving.

*DANCING WITH ISLAM'S ASSASSINS*

According to an article on the CDC website, "The potential threat of biological warfare with a specific agent is proportional to the susceptibility of the population to that agent. Preventing disease after exposure to a biological agent is partially a function of the immunity of the exposed individual."[161] In other words, the better your immune system, the less likely you are to die in a given epidemic—even a man-made epidemic. In every epidemic, some people who are exposed to that particular disease will live, while others will die. What makes the difference? Often, it is the strength of the exposed person's immune system.

The best thing you can do to prepare your family to survive a biological attack is to ensure that everyone in your family is in the best possible health and the best possible shape. This is something that will stand you in good stead even if you are never attacked by terrorists, but in case of a terrorist attack, it can be the difference between life and death. Get into the best shape possible for you: you never know when the ability to run down flights of stairs or away from a burning building will become just as important in your own life as it was to the occupants of the Twin Towers on 9/11. Nor do you know when maintaining a healthy lifestyle may keep you from coming down with a dread disease disseminated by some terrorist. So eat right, take your vitamins, get enough sleep, and be sure to exercise. Do all the common-sense things you know to do to stay as healthy and fit as possible, because your life will not only be enhanced by it—it may actually depend on it.

Another common-sense thing you can do is to rid your house and yard of insects and rodents. Mosquitoes, fleas, ticks, lice, and rodents are the natural carriers ("reservoirs") of many diseases that are likely to be used as weapons of mass destruction. Once these diseases are loose in your environment, they can lodge in these natural reservoirs and spread from them to you.

## Which Biological Agents Are Most Dangerous?

According to the Centers for Disease Control and

Prevention website:

> The Centers for Disease Control and Prevention classifies agents with recognized bioterrorism potential into three priority areas (A, B and C).... Category A agents are those that:
>
> - pose the greatest possible threat for a bad effect on public health
>
> - may spread across a large area or need public awareness
>
> - need a great deal of planning to protect the public's health [162]

The Category A agents are as follows: Bacillus anthracis (anthrax), Clostridium botulinum (botulism), Yersinia pestis (plague), Variola major (smallpox) and other pox viruses, Francisella tularensis (tularemia), and viral hemorrhagic fevers.

There are too many biological agents out there for me to detail all of them, but the rest of this chapter lists the Category A threats and their symptoms, so that you will know what to watch out for. As I am not a doctor, most of this information came from various pages on the CDC website.

## Bacillus anthracis (anthrax)

### What are the symptoms of anthrax? [163]

Symptoms of disease vary depending on how the disease was contracted, but symptoms usually occur within 7 days.

*Cutaneous:* Most (about 95%) anthrax infections occur when the bacterium enters a cut or abrasion on the skin, such as when handling contaminated wool, hides, leather or hair products (especially goat hair) of infected animals. Skin infection begins as a raised itchy bump that resembles an insect bite but within 1-2 days develops into a vesicle and then a painless ulcer, usually 1-3 cm in diameter, with a characteristic black necrotic (dying) area in the center. Lymph glands in the adjacent area may swell. About 20% of untreated cases of cutaneous anthrax will result in death. Deaths are rare with appropriate antimicrobial therapy.

*inhalation:* Initial symptoms may resemble a common cold. After several days, the symptoms may progress to severe breathing problems and shock. inhalation anthrax is usually fatal.

*Intestinal:* The intestinal disease form of anthrax may follow the consumption of contaminated meat and is characterized by an acute inflammation of the intestinal tract. Initial signs of nausea, loss of appetite, vomiting, fever are followed by abdominal pain, vomiting of blood, and severe diarrhea. Intestinal anthrax results in death in 25% to 60% of cases.

## *Clostridium botulinum* (botulism)

Botulism is a paralytic illness caused by a nerve toxin that is produced by the bacterium *Clostridium botulinum*. There are three main kinds: foodborne, wound botulism, and infant botulism. Infant botulism is caused by consuming the spores of the botulinum bacteria; foodborne botulism is caused by eating foods that contain the toxin produced by the botulinum bacteria, and wound botulism is caused when a wound becomes infected with the botulinum bacteria. The botulism toxin is destroyed by high temperatures. Foodborne botulism can be prevented by boiling food for 10 minutes before eating it.

### What are the symptoms of botulism? [164]

The classic symptoms of botulism include double vision, blurred vision, drooping eyelids, slurred speech, difficulty swallowing, dry mouth, and muscle weakness. Infants with botulism appear lethargic, feed poorly, are constipated, and have a weak cry and poor muscle tone. These are all symptoms of the muscle paralysis caused by the bacterial toxin. If untreated, these symptoms may progress to cause paralysis of the arms, legs, trunk and respiratory muscles. In foodborne botulism, symptoms generally begin 18 to 36 hours after eating a contaminated food, but they can occur as early as 6 hours or as late as 10 days.

## *Yersinia pestis* (plague)

### Clinical Features[165]

- **Bubonic plague:** enlarged, tender lymph nodes, fever, chills and prostration
- **Septicemic plague:** fever, chills, prostration, abdominal pain, shock and bleeding into skin and other organs
- **Pneumonic plague:** fever, chills, cough and difficulty breathing; rapid shock and death if not treated early

### Diagnosis[166]

The typical sign of the most common form of human plague is a swollen and very tender lymph gland, accompanied by pain. The swollen gland is called a "bubo." Bubonic plague should be suspected when a person develops a swollen gland, fever, chills, headache, and extreme exhaustion, and has a history of possible exposure to infected rodents, rabbits, or fleas. A person usually becomes ill with bubonic plague 2 to 6 days after being infected.

When bubonic plague is left untreated, plague bacteria invade the bloodstream. As the plague bacteria multiply in the bloodstream, they spread rapidly throughout the body and cause a severe and often fatal condition. Infection of the lungs with the plague bacterium causes the pneumonic form of plague, a severe respiratory illness. The infected person may experience high fever, chills, cough, and breathing difficulty and may expel bloody sputum. If plague patients are not given specific antibiotic therapy, the disease can progress rapidly to death. About 14% (1 in 7) of all plague cases in the United States are fatal.

# *Variola major* (smallpox) and other pox viruses

## *Smallpox Disease Overview*[167]

### The Disease

Smallpox is a serious, contagious, and sometimes fatal infectious disease. There is no specific treatment for smallpox disease, and the only prevention is vaccination. The name smallpox is derived from the Latin word for "spotted" and refers to the raised bumps that appear on the face and body of an infected person.

There are two clinical forms of smallpox. Variola major is the severe and most common form of smallpox, with a more extensive rash and higher fever. There are four types of variola major smallpox: ordinary (the most frequent type, accounting for 90% or more of cases); modified (mild and occurring in previously vaccinated persons); flat; and hemorrhagic (both rare and very severe). Historically, variola major has an overall fatality rate of about 30%; however, flat and hemorrhagic smallpox usually are fatal. Variola minor is a less common presentation of smallpox, and a much less severe disease, with death rates historically of 1% or less.

Smallpox outbreaks have occurred from time to time for thousands of years, but the disease is now eradicated after a successful worldwide vaccination program. The last case of smallpox in the United States was in 1949. The last naturally occurring case in the world was in Somalia in 1977. After the disease was eliminated from the world, routine vaccination against smallpox among the general public was stopped because it was no longer necessary for prevention.

### Transmission

Generally, direct and fairly prolonged face-to-face contact is required to spread smallpox from one person to another. Smallpox also can be spread through direct contact with infected bodily fluids or contaminated objects such as bedding or clothing. Rarely, smallpox has been spread by virus carried in the air in enclosed settings such as buildings, buses, and trains. Humans are the only natural hosts of variola. Smallpox is not known to be transmitted by insects or animals.

A person with smallpox is sometimes contagious with onset of fever (prodrome phase), but the person becomes most contagious with the onset of rash. At this stage the infected person is usually very sick and not able to move around in the community. The infected person is contagious until the last smallpox scab falls off.

### Smallpox Disease

| | |
|---|---|
| **Incubation Period (Duration: 7 to 17 days)** *Not contagious* | **Exposure to the virus** is followed by an incubation period during which people do not have any symptoms and may feel fine. This incubation period averages about 12 to 14 days but can range from 7 to 17 days. During this time, people are not contagious. |
| **Initial Symptoms** *(Prodrome)* **(Duration: 2 to 4 days)** *Sometimes contagious\** | The **first symptoms** of smallpox include fever, malaise, head and body aches, and sometimes vomiting. The fever is usually high, in the range of 101 to 104 degrees Fahrenheit. At this time, people are usually too sick to carry on their normal activities. This is called the *prodrome* phase and may last for 2 to 4 days. |

| | |
|---|---|
| **Early Rash** <br> **(Duration:** <br> **about 4 days)** <br> *Most contagious* <br><br> . | A **rash emerges** first as small red spots on the tongue and in the mouth. <br><br> These spots develop into sores that break open and spread large amounts of the virus into the mouth and throat. At this time, the person becomes **most contagious**. <br><br> Around the time the sores in the mouth break down, a rash appears on the skin, starting on the face and spreading to the arms and legs and then to the hands and feet. Usually the rash spreads to all parts of the body within 24 hours. As the rash appears, the fever usually falls and the person may start to feel better. <br><br> By the third day of the rash, the rash becomes raised bumps. <br><br> By the fourth day, the bumps fill with a thick, opaque fluid and often have a depression in the center that looks like a bellybutton. (This is a major distinguishing characteristic of smallpox.) <br><br> Fever often will rise again at this time and remain high until scabs form over the bumps. |
| **Pustular Rash** <br> **(Duration:** <br> **about 5 days)** <br> *Contagious* | The bumps become **pustules**—sharply raised, usually round and firm to the touch as if there's a small round object under the skin. People often say the bumps feel like BB pellets embedded in the skin. |

| | |
|---|---|
| **Pustules and Scabs (Duration: about 5 days)** *Contagious* | The pustules begin to form a crust and then **scab**.<br><br>By the end of the second week after the rash appears, most of the sores have scabbed over. |
| **Resolving Scabs (Duration: about 6 days)** *Contagious* | The scabs begin to fall off, leaving marks on the skin that eventually become pitted **scars**. Most scabs will have fallen off three weeks after the rash appears.<br><br>The person is contagious to others until all of the scabs have fallen off. |
| **Scabs resolved** *Not contagious* | Scabs have fallen off. Person is no longer contagious. |

\* Smallpox may be contagious during the *prodrome* phase, but is most infectious during the first 7 to 10 days following rash onset.

## *Francisella tularensis* (tularemia)

### What are the Symptoms of Tularemia?[168]

Symptoms of tularemia could include:

- sudden fever
- chills
- headaches
- diarrhea
- muscle aches
- joint pain
- dry cough
- progressive weakness

177

People can also catch pneumonia and develop chest pain, bloody sputum and can have trouble breathing and even sometimes stop breathing.

Other symptoms of tularemia depend on how a person was exposed to the tularemia bacteria. These symptoms can include ulcers on the skin or mouth, swollen and painful lymph glands, swollen and painful eyes, and a sore throat.

## How Does Tularemia Spread?

People can get tularemia many different ways:

- being bitten by an infected tick, deerfly or other insect
- handling infected animal carcasses
- eating or drinking contaminated food or water
- breathing in the bacteria, *F. tularensis*

Tularemia is not known to be spread from person to person. People who have tularemia do not need to be isolated. People who have been exposed to the tularemia bacteria should be treated as soon as possible. The disease can be fatal if it is not treated with the right antibiotics.

## How Soon Do Infected People Get Sick?

Symptoms usually appear 3 to 5 days after exposure to the bacteria, but can take as long as 14 days.

# Viral Hemorrhagic Fevers

Viral hemorrhagic fevers include Arenaviruses (LCM, Junin virus, Machupo virus, Guanarito virus, Lassa Fever), Bunyaviruses (Hantaviruses, Rift Valley Fever), Flaviviruses (Dengue) and Filoviruses (Ebola, Marburg). The hosts for these viruses are usually rodents, ticks, and mosquitoes, although the hosts for Ebola and Marburg are unknown.

## What are the symptoms of viral hemorrhagic fever illnesses?[169]

Specific signs and symptoms vary by the type of VHF, but initial signs and symptoms often include marked fever, fatigue, dizziness, muscle aches, loss of strength, and exhaustion. Patients with severe cases of VHF often show signs of bleeding under the skin, in internal organs, or from body orifices like the mouth, eyes, or ears. However, although they may bleed from many sites around the body, patients rarely die because of blood loss. Severely ill patient cases may also show shock, nervous system malfunction, coma, delirium, and seizures. Some types of VHF are associated with renal (kidney) failure.

## How are patients with viral hemorrhagic fever treated?[170]

Patients receive supportive therapy, but generally speaking, there is no other treatment or established cure for VHFs. Ribavirin, an anti-viral drug, has been effective in treating some individuals with Lassa fever or HFRS. Treatment with convalescent-phase plasma has been used with success in some patients with Argentine hemorrhagic fever.

# CHAPTER 20

# HOW TO PROTECT YOUR FAMILY FROM NUCLEAR ATTACK

Surviving a nuclear attack has a lot to do with how close you are to ground zero and the size of the nuclear device that was detonated. Assuming that terrorists would be most likely to use a "suitcase bomb," deaths at ground zero would be 100%, 98% at ½ mile, 50% at one mile (with 50% severe injuries), 15% at two miles (with severe injuries at 25%) and 5% at three miles (with 25% moderate injuries). Beyond three miles, fallout is the greatest hazard.[171]

Radioactive fallout is the dust produced by a nuclear explosion. It is carried by the wind, so most of it settles back to earth downwind of the blast. The heaviest dust will "fall out" first, closest to ground zero, while the smaller, lighter particles can be carried much father downwind, often several hundred miles, typically arriving hours after the blast.

Inhaling radioactive fallout is by far the most lethal kind of exposure. Painting masks and other "dust masks" don't provide protection against radioactive particulates—here again, you will want to make sure your family is equipped with NBC-rated gas masks. Since fallout can be washed from the skin but cannot be removed from the lungs, a gas mask is the most important piece of equipment to have on hand during a nuclear emergency.

While the fallout itself may stay outside, the radiation it carries can go right through walls, roofs, and protective clothing. However, fallout will lose 90% of its energy in the first three days and 99% within two weeks.

The following information on protecting yourself during and after a nuclear blast is from FEMA's Are You Ready website.[172] It contains a lot of excellent information, but once again it fails to mention the use of NBC gas masks and protective suits.

### Radioactive Fallout

Even if individuals are not close enough to the nuclear blast to be affected by the direct impacts, they may be affected by radioactive fallout. Any nuclear blast results in some fallout. Blasts that occur near the earth's surface create much greater amounts of fallout than blasts that occur at higher altitudes. This is because the tremendous heat produced from a nuclear blast causes an up-draft of air that forms the familiar mushroom cloud. When a blast occurs near the earth's surface, millions of vaporized dirt particles also are drawn into the cloud. As the heat diminishes, radioactive materials that have vaporized condense on the particles and fall back to Earth. The phenomenon is called radioactive fallout. This fallout material decays over a long period of time, and is the main source of residual nuclear radiation.

Fallout from a nuclear explosion may be carried by wind currents for hundreds of miles if the right conditions exist. Effects from even a small portable device exploded at ground level can be potentially deadly.

Nuclear radiation cannot be seen, smelled, or otherwise detected by normal senses. Radiation can only be detected by radiation monitoring devices. This makes radiological emergencies different from other types of emergencies, such as floods or hurricanes. Monitoring can project the fallout arrival times, which will be announced through official warning channels. However, any increase in surface build-up of gritty dust and dirt should be a warning for taking protective measures.

### Radioactive Fallout [sic]

In addition to other effects, a nuclear weapon detonated in or above the earth's atmosphere can create an electromagnetic pulse (EMP), a high-density electrical field. An EMP acts like a stroke of lightning but is stronger, faster, and shorter. An EMP can seriously damage electronic devices connected to power sources or antennas. This includes communication systems, computers, electrical appliances, and automobile or aircraft ignition systems. The damage could range from a minor interruption to actual burnout of components. Most electronic equipment within 1,000 miles of a high-altitude nuclear detonation could be affected. Battery-powered radios with short antennas generally would not be affected. Although an EMP is unlikely to harm most people, it could harm those with pacemakers or other implanted electronic devices.

### Protection from a Nuclear Blast

The danger of a massive strategic nuclear attack on the United States is predicted by experts to be less likely today. However, terrorism, by nature, is unpredictable.

If there were threat of an attack, people living near potential targets could be advised to evacuate or they could decide on their own to evacuate to an area not considered a likely target. Protection from radioactive fallout would require taking shelter in an underground area or in the middle of a large building.

In general, potential targets include:

- Strategic missile sites and military bases.
- Centers of government such as Washington, DC, and state capitals.
- Important transportation and communication centers.
- Manufacturing, industrial, technology, and financial centers.
- Petroleum refineries, electrical power plants, and chemical plants.
- Major ports and airfields.

The three factors for protecting oneself from radiation and fallout are distance, shielding, and time.

- Distance - the more distance between you and the fallout particles, the better. An underground area such as a home or office building basement offers more protection than the first floor of a building. A floor near the middle of a high-rise may be better, depending on what is nearby at that level on which significant fallout particles would collect. Flat roofs collect fallout particles so the top floor is not a good choice, nor is a floor adjacent to a neighboring flat roof.
- Shielding - the heavier and denser the materials - thick

walls, concrete, bricks, books and earth - between you and the fallout particles, the better.

- Time - fallout radiation loses its intensity fairly rapidly. In time, you will be able to leave the fallout shelter. Radioactive fallout poses the greatest threat to people during the first two weeks, by which time it has declined to about 1 percent of its initial radiation level.

Remember that any protection, however temporary, is better than none at all, and the more shielding, distance, and time you can take advantage of, the better.

## Take Protective Measures

### Before a Nuclear Blast

To prepare for a nuclear blast, you should do the following:

- Find out from officials if any public buildings in your community have been designated as fallout shelters. If none have been designated, make your own list of potential shelters near your home, workplace, and school. These places would include basements or the windowless center area of middle floors in high-rise buildings, as well as subways and tunnels.
- If you live in an apartment building or high-rise, talk to the manager about the safest place in the building for sheltering and about providing for building occupants until it is safe to go out.
- During periods of increased threat increase your disaster supplies to be adequate for up to two weeks.

Taking shelter during a nuclear blast is absolutely necessary. There are two kinds of shelters - blast and fallout. The following describes the two kinds of shelters:

- Blast shelters are specifically constructed to offer some

protection against blast pressure, initial radiation, heat, and fire. But even a blast shelter cannot withstand a direct hit from a nuclear explosion.

- Fallout shelters do not need to be specially constructed for protecting against fallout. They can be any protected space, provided that the walls and roof are thick and dense enough to absorb the radiation given off by fallout particles.

### During a Nuclear Blast

The following are guidelines for what to do in the event of a nuclear explosion.

If an attack warning is issued:

- Take cover as quickly as you can, below ground if possible, and stay there until instructed to do otherwise.
- Listen for official information and follow instructions.

If you are caught outside and unable to get inside immediately:

- Do not look at the flash or fireball - it can blind you.
- Take cover behind anything that might offer protection.
- Lie flat on the ground and cover your head. If the explosion is some distance away, it could take 3 0 seconds or more for the blast wave to hit.
- Take shelter as soon as you can, even if you are many miles from ground zero where the attack occurred - radioactive fallout can be carried by the winds for hundreds of miles.

Remember the three protective factors: Distance, shielding, and time.

### After a Nuclear Blast

Decay rates of the radioactive fallout are the same for any size nuclear device. However, the amount of fallout will vary based on the size of the device and its proximity to the ground. Therefore, it might be necessary for those in the areas with highest radiation levels to shelter for up to a month.

The heaviest fallout would be limited to the area at or downwind from the explosion, and 80 percent of the fallout would occur during the first 24 hours.

People in most of the areas that would be affected could be allowed to come out of shelter within a few days and, if necessary, evacuate to unaffected areas.

## Potassium Iodide

Potassium iodide (chemical symbol: KI) is a well-known blocker of thyroid radioiodine uptake. When the proper dose is taken in a timely manner, potassium iodide reduces the risk of thyroid cancer in people who have inhaled or ingested radioiodines. Potassium iodide works by flooding the thyroid with non-radioactive iodine and preventing the uptake of the radioactive molecules, which are then excreted in the urine. Potassium Iodide won't protect you against other radiation hazards, but it will greatly reduce your risk of developing thyroid cancer later in life. It is very inexpensive and should definitely be included among your emergency supplies.

### KI Use in Radiation Emergencies: Treatment Recommendations[173]

After careful review of the data from Chernobyl relating estimated thyroid radiation dose and cancer risk in exposed children, FDA is revising its recommendation for administration of KI based on age, predicted thyroid exposure, and pregnancy and lactation status (see Table).

| Threshold Thyroid Radioactive Exposures and Recommended Doses of KI for Different Risk Groups | | | | |
|---|---|---|---|---|
| | Predicted Thyroid exposure(cGy) | KI dose (mg) | # of 130 mg tablets | # of 65 mg tablets |
| Adults over 40 yrs | ≥500 | 130 | 1 | 2 |
| Adults over 18 through 40 yrs | ≥10 | | | |
| Pregnant or lactating women | ≥ 5 | | | |
| Adolescents. over 12 through 18 yrs* | | 65 | 1/2 | 1 |
| Children over 3 through 12 yrs | | | | |
| Over 1 month through 3 years | | 32 | 1/4 | 1/2 |
| Birth through 1 month | | 16 | 1/8 | 1/4 |

*Adolescents approaching adult size ($\geq$ 70 kg) should receive the full adult dose (130 mg).

The protective effect of KI lasts approximately 24 hours. For optimal prophylaxis, KI should therefore be dosed daily, until a risk of significant exposure to radioiodines by either inhalation or ingestion no longer exists. Individuals intolerant of KI at protective doses, and neonates, pregnant and lactating women (in whom repeat administration of KI raises particular safety issues, see below) should be given priority with regard to other protective measures (i.e., sheltering, evacuation, and control of the food supply).

Note that adults over 40 need take KI only in the case of a projected large internal radiation dose to the thyroid (>500 cGy) to prevent hypothyroidism.

These recommendations are meant to provide states and local authorities as well as other agencies with the best current guidance on safe and effective use of KI to reduce thyroidal radioiodine exposure and thus the risk of thyroid cancer. FDA recognizes that, in the event of an emergency, some or all of the specific dosing recommendations may be very difficult to carry out given their complexity and the logistics of implementation of a program of KI distribution. The recommendations should therefore be interpreted with flexibility as necessary to allow optimally effective and safe dosing given the exigencies of any particular emergency situation. In this context, we offer the following critical general guidance: *across populations at risk for radioiodine exposure, the overall benefits of KI far exceed the risks of overdosing, especially in children, though we continue to emphasize particular attention to dose in infants.*

# CHAPTER 21

# SUPERNATURAL PROTECTION

This book contains a number of natural steps you can take to protect yourself in time of enemy attack or natural disaster. It would be incomplete if we didn't tell you about some supernatural steps you can take as well.

The Bible teaches that you don't have to be particularly wicked to have bad things happen to you:

> There were present at that season some that told him of the Galilaeans, whose blood Pilate had mingled with their sacrifices. And Jesus answering said unto them, Suppose ye that these Galilaeans were sinners above all the Galilaeans, because they suffered such things? I tell you, Nay: but, except ye repent, ye shall all likewise perish. Or those eighteen, upon whom the tower in Siloam fell, and slew them, think ye that they were sinners above all men that dwelt in Jerusalem? I tell you, Nay: but, except ye repent, ye shall all likewise perish.
>
> Luke 13:1-5

The Bible also teaches that there is a place of supernatural protection for the saints of God. Perhaps one of the best-known passages on God's supernatural protection is Psalm 91. Verse 1 says, "He that dwelleth in the secret place of the most High shall abide under the shadow of the Almighty." To claim this particular Bible promise, you need to "dwell in the secret place of the most High." You need to be close to God—close enough to be under His shadow. There is a similar thought in Psalm 57:1, "Be merciful unto me, O God, be merciful unto me: for my soul trusteth in thee: yea, in the shadow of thy wings will I make my refuge, until *these* calamities be overpast."

Not only do you need to dwell close to God, but you need to explicitly put your faith in Him. Verse 2 says, "I will say of the LORD, *He is* my refuge and my fortress: my God; in him will I trust."

*If* you are close to God, and *if* you place your trust in Him, then the Bible tells us, in the rest of this Psalm, that you can expect to experience God's supernatural protection in times of trouble:

> Surely he shall deliver thee from the snare of the fowler, *and* from the noisome pestilence. He shall cover thee with his feathers, and under his wings shalt thou trust: his truth *shall be thy* shield and buckler. Thou shalt not be afraid for the terror by night; *nor* for the arrow *that* flieth by day; *Nor* for the pestilence *that* walketh in darkness; *nor* for the destruction *that* wasteth at noonday. A thousand shall fall at thy side, and ten thousand at thy right hand; *but* it shall not come nigh thee. Only with thine eyes shalt thou behold and see the reward of the wicked. Because thou hast made the LORD, *which is* my refuge, *even* the most High, thy habitation; There shall no evil befall thee, neither shall any plague come nigh thy dwelling. For he shall give his angels charge over thee, to keep thee in all thy ways. They shall bear thee up in *their* hands, lest thou dash thy foot against a stone. Thou shalt

tread upon the lion and adder: the young lion and the dragon shalt thou trample under feet. Because he hath set his love upon me, therefore will I deliver him: I will set him on high, because he hath known my name. He shall call upon me, and I will answer him: I *will be* with him in trouble; I will deliver him, and honour him. With long life will I satisfy him, and shew him my salvation.

Psalm 91:3-16

If you make God your habitation, Psalm 91 teaches, "there shall no evil befall these." What does it mean to make God your habitation? In John 15:1-10, Jesus taught that we should "abide" in Him. To "abide" is to dwell. If you dwell somewhere, you make it your habitation. Here's what Jesus had to say about abiding:

I am the true vine, and my Father is the husbandman. Every branch in me that beareth not fruit he taketh away: and every *branch* that beareth fruit, he purgeth it, that it may bring forth more fruit. Now ye are clean through the word which I have spoken unto you. Abide in me, and I in you. As the branch cannot bear fruit of itself, except it abide in the vine; no more can ye, except ye abide in me. I am the vine, ye *are* the branches: He that abideth in me, and I in him, the same bringeth forth much fruit: for without me ye can do nothing. If a man abide not in me, he is cast forth as a branch, and is withered; and men gather them, and cast *them* into the fire, and they are burned. If ye abide in me, and my words abide in you, ye shall ask what ye will, and it shall be done unto you. Herein is my Father glorified, that ye bear much fruit; so shall ye be my disciples. As the Father hath loved me, so have I loved you: continue ye in my love. If ye keep my commandments, ye shall abide in my love; even as I have kept my Father's commandments, and abide in his love.

Christians, we cannot depend on a one-time prayer to save us from disaster, either physically or spiritually. Christianity is meant to be an ongoing relationship with Christ. If we abide in Him, we bring forth much fruit. If we abide in Him *and* His words abide in us, He will answer our prayers. If a so-called Christian does *not* abide in Him, "he is cast forth as a branch, and is withered; and men gather them, and cast *them* into the fire, and they are burned." I'm not going to argue theology here—I'm just telling you what the Bible says.

There is a place in God where you abide in God and God's words abide in you. Romans 10:17 says, "So then faith *cometh* by hearing, and hearing by the word of God." When you abide in God and His words abide in you, faith cometh by hearing.

In Hebrews 11:32-34, the Bible tells us about believers who, through faith, were delivered out of harm's way: "And what shall I more say? for the time would fail me to tell of Gedeon, and of Barak, and of Samson, and of Jephthae; of David also, and Samuel, and of the prophets: Who through faith subdued kingdoms, wrought righteousness, obtained promises, stopped the mouths of lions, Quenched the violence of fire, escaped the edge of the sword, out of weakness were made strong, waxed valiant in fight, turned to flight the armies of the aliens."

Does God still work miracles today? Absolutely! I have seen God work many mighty miracles, both in my own life and in my healing crusades. Can people be divinely protected from terrorist attacks strictly through faith? Absolutely! So here's my supernatural "How To" list for praying the prayer of faith for yourself and your family:

- Be sure you're dwelling in the secret place of the Most High.
- Abide in Christ—live right and maintain your relationship with Him.
- Let His Words abide in you—Meditate on the Word of God.
- In time of crisis, ***don't forget to pray!***

# CHAPTER 22

# THE KING IS AT THE DOOR

As you can tell by what I said in the previous chapter, I believe we are living in what the Bible calls the last days. Actually, I believe that we are living in the very last of the last days.

> When he was sitting on the Mount of Olives, the disciples came to him privately, saying, "Tell us, when will this be, and what will be the sign of your coming and of the end of the age?" Jesus answered them, "Beware that no one leads you astray. For many will come in my name, saying, 'I am the Messiah!' and they will lead many astray. And you will hear of wars and rumors of wars; see that you are not alarmed; for this must take place, but the end is not yet. For nation will rise against nation, and kingdom against kingdom, and there will be famines and earthquakes in various places: all this is but the beginning of the birth pangs.
>
> Matthew 24:3 - 8 (NRSV)

The Birth Pangs that Jesus spoke about two thousand years ago are coming to pass right now, in our lifetimes. Things that seem strange to us aren't strange according to the Bible. We are living in the end times. The tsunami in Indonesia, the floods in California, the unusual arctic cold fronts, Hurricanes Katrina and Rita, terrorist attacks, wars and rumors of wars, and other disasters that are yet to come—these are nothing but what the Bible calls birth pangs: the suffering that is necessary before a new world can be born.

Yes, there have always been disasters. Yes, there have always been floods. Yes, terrifying events have taken place in every age. The difference in what's happening today is the frequency of these events and their worldwide distribution.

The emphasis of this book has been on terrorists, but for the majority of people, terrorists aren't what they really need to fear. Natural disasters aren't what they really need to fear. What *should* they fear? Jesus said, "And fear not them which kill the body, but are not able to kill the soul: but rather fear him which is able to destroy both soul and body in hell" (Matthew 10:28).

Jesus tells us: DON'T be afraid of dying; DO be afraid of going to hell.

Just before He raised Lazarus from the dead, Jesus told Lazarus' sister Martha, "I am the resurrection, and the life: he that believeth in me, though he were dead, yet shall he live: And whosoever liveth and believeth in me shall never die" (John 11:25-26).

It is a fact of life that since the world began almost all of us have been born to die. Yes, the Bible does talk about Enoch and Elijah, both of whom were bodily "caught up" at the end of their lives, without actually dying as we know it. And when Jesus returns for His Church, the Bible tells us that everyone who is in Christ—whether dead or alive—will be "caught up" to meet Him in the clouds:

> But I would not have you to be ignorant, brethren, concerning them which are asleep, that ye sorrow not, even as others which have no hope. For if we believe that Jesus died and rose again, even so them

also which sleep in Jesus will God bring with him. For this we say unto you by the word of the Lord, that we which are alive and remain unto the coming of the Lord shall not prevent them which are asleep. For the Lord himself shall descend from heaven with a shout, with the voice of the archangel, and with the trump of God: and the dead in Christ shall rise first: Then we which are alive and remain shall be caught up together with them in the clouds, to meet the Lord in the air: and so shall we ever be with the Lord. Wherefore comfort one another with these words.

1 Thessalonians 4:13-18

For the Christian, death isn't something to fear. If our mortal bodies die, our consciousness lives on. Our souls and spirits never die, and God has prepared immortal bodies for all believers. Paul writes:

Behold, I show you a mystery; We shall not all sleep, but we shall all be changed, In a moment, in the twinkling of an eye, at the last trump: for the trumpet shall sound, and the dead shall be raised incorruptible, and we shall be changed. For this corruptible must put on incorruption, and this mortal must put on immortality. So when this corruptible shall have put on incorruption, and this mortal shall have put on immortality, then shall be brought to pass the saying that is written, Death is swallowed up in victory. O death, where is thy sting? O grave, where is thy victory? The sting of death is sin; and the strength of sin is the law. But thanks be to God, which giveth us the victory through our Lord Jesus Christ.

1 Corinthians 15:51-57

If you know God, there is no reason to be afraid of death.

God, who even cares when a sparrow dies, cares very much more for you. But if you don't know Christ, a terrible fate awaits you when you die. Jesus said:

> And if thy hand offend thee, cut it off: it is better for thee to enter into life maimed, than having two hands to go into hell, into the fire that never shall be quenched: Where their worm dieth not, and the fire is not quenched. And if thy foot offend thee, cut it off: it is better for thee to enter halt into life, than having two feet to be cast into hell, into the fire that never shall be quenched: Where their worm dieth not, and the fire is not quenched. And if thine eye offend thee, pluck it out: it is better for thee to enter into the kingdom of God with one eye, than having two eyes to be cast into hell fire: Where their worm dieth not, and the fire is not quenched.
>
> Mark 9:43-48

You say you don't believe in hell? Jesus believes in it! As we will see, you don't actually need to cut off your hand or pluck out your eye to escape the fires of hell; what Jesus is saying here is that *if you had to*, it would be worth it! It would be worth paying any price you had to pay—it would be worth spending every day of this finite earthly life in misery—to escape spending eternity in torment that lasts forever. Compared to "forever," your earthly life amounts to less than a blink of the eye. The Good News of the Gospel is that you don't *have* to spend your earthly life in misery in order to escape the fires of hell. God wants His children to be blessed, not cursed. But *if you had to*, it would be worth it.

I wouldn't be much of a preacher if I told you how to save your physical body from terrorists and other earthly threats, but didn't tell you how to save your eternal life, and I want you to know that if you aren't saved, the best thing you can do is drop everything, and turn right now to Page 261, where you can find "Six Scriptural Steps to Salvation" that will tell you exactly what you need to do to be saved. No matter what else you accomplish here on earth, making sure of your salvation is the most important thing you will ever do in life.

This chapter is entitled "The King Is at the Door," and I began this chapter by saying that we are living in a time of birth pangs.

The Bible has a lot to say about the things that will happen in what it calls "the latter days." One of the things we can expect to happen in the very near future is "the day of the Lord."

Let's look at the Prophecy of Joel:

> Alas for the day! for the day of the LORD is at hand, and as a destruction from the Almighty shall it come. Is not the meat cut off before our eyes, yea, joy and gladness from the house of our God? The seed is rotten under their clods, the garners are laid desolate, the barns are broken down; for the corn is withered. How do the beasts groan! the herds of cattle are perplexed, because they have no pasture; yea, the flocks of sheep are made desolate. O LORD, to thee will I cry: for the fire hath devoured the pastures of the wilderness, and the flame hath burned all the trees of the field. The beasts of the field cry also unto thee: for the rivers of waters are dried up, and the fire hath devoured the pastures of the wilderness. Blow ye the trumpet in Zion, and sound an alarm in my holy mountain: let all the inhabitants of the land tremble: for the day of the LORD cometh, for it is nigh at hand;
>
> Joel 1:15-2:1

I particularly wish to draw your attention to the first verse of the second chapter.

"Blow ye the trumpet in Zion and sound an alarm in my holy mountain: let all the inhabitants of the land tremble; for the day of the Lord cometh, for it is nigh at hand."

When I compare current events with the end-time

prophecies of the Bible, it is easy for me to see that we are living in the very last of the last days. If this is the case, what should we do?

Joel said, "Let the priests, the ministers of the Lord weep between the porch and the alter, and let them say, spare thy people, O Lord and give not thine heritage to reproach that the heathen should rule over them. Wherefore should they say among the people, Where is their God?"

Where is their God?

If ever there was a day when that question should be asked it is now.

What do people see when we look at the Church? In all too many cases, what they see is a church robbed of its power, a church divested of the glory of the presence of the Lord, a church without an altar, a church that has deteriorated until it is nothing more than a social club keeping itself together by the introduction of ethical systems, a church that has absolutely lost the confidence of the people of the world.

On every hand people are saying, "Where is their God?" Is it any wonder that people flee their dead Christian churches? What is the reason for this exodus of people from the so-called church into every bloodless cult and Crossless creed? I will tell you why. SATISFIED SHEEP do not go looking around for new pastures.

I am thoroughly persuaded that if God's flock were satisfied we would never have to hold a convention and talk about an exodus.

If people had churches where the Gospel of Jesus Christ was really preached; if they knew the power of the Blood of Jesus, if they had churches where the Cross was exalted, and—most important of all—if people had churches where they could experience a true born again experience, they would be satisfied.

Nobody eats garbage when they could be eating wholesome food.

Paul wrote, "And my speech and my preaching *was* not with enticing words of man's wisdom, but in demonstration of the Spirit and of power: That your faith should not stand in the wisdom of men, but in the power of God" (1 Corinthians 2:4-5).

Nobody leaves a church where people are born again and the power of God is manifested.

Once Jesus ascended into heaven, anyone could get saved. "For there is no difference between the Jew and the Greek: for the same Lord over all is rich unto all that call upon him. For whosoever shall call upon the name of the Lord shall be saved." (Romans 10:12-13). But when He was on earth, Jesus was sent to preach to the Jews:

> Then Jesus went thence, and departed into the coasts of Tyre and Sidon. And, behold, a woman of Canaan came out of the same coasts, and cried unto him, saying, Have mercy on me, O Lord, thou Son of David; my daughter is grievously vexed with a devil. But he answered her not a word. And his disciples came and besought him, saying, Send her away; for she crieth after us. But he answered and said, I am not sent but unto the lost sheep of the house of Israel. Then came she and worshipped him, saying, Lord, help me. But he answered and said, It is not meet to take the children's bread, and to cast it to dogs. And she said, Truth, Lord: yet the dogs eat of the crumbs which fall from their masters' table. Then Jesus answered and said unto her, O woman, great is thy faith: be it unto thee even as thou wilt. And her daughter was made whole from that very hour.
>
> Matthew 15:21-28

Paul preached "in demonstration of the Spirit and of power"; Before Paul, Jesus had also preached in demonstration of the Spirit and of power—and he called that kind of power "the children's bread." Miracle-working power is "the children's bread." Miracle-working power *belongs* to the believer. It *belongs* to the children of God.

In the Book of John, Jesus said, "I am the living bread

which came down from heaven: if any man eat of this bread, he shall live for ever:" (John 6:50a).

People who are suffering from starvation will eat almost anything, even garbage. People who have been satisfied with the living bread from heaven will not be interested in eating spiritual garbage. If the Gospel Jesus Christ were really proclaimed; if the blood were preached, if the Cross were exalted, if a born again experience became the possession of every seeker at the altar, then there would be satisfaction in the churches. Then people would not go out seeking new pastures; you could not drive them out!

We need to return to the old-time Gospel, and we need to do it now. "Blow ye the trumpet to Zion ... for THE DAY OF THE LORD ... IS NIGH AT HAND.

The day is at hand!

Joel was not speaking here of the first coming of the Lord Jesus Christ. A great many people are astonished to find that the Old Testament is filled with prophecies relative to the second coming of Jesus, when we he will come in the clouds of glory, bringing His saints with Him. Jude 1:4 tells us that "Enoch also, the seventh from Adam, prophesied of these, saying, Behold, the Lord cometh with ten thousands of his saints." Enoch was one of the first Old Testament prophets, so we know from Jude that the prophets of God were aware of the Second Coming of Jesus as early as Enoch.

Nobody owns the future. Nobody can say that they won't die today—in an automobile accident, in a plane crash, of a heart attack, at the hands of a terrorist. And nobody can tell you when Jesus is coming back. But while nobody can tell *when* his earthly life will end, everyone who hears the gospel can make certain of *where* he will spend eternity.

Have you ever sinned? I happen to know that you have. This is because the Bible says "All we like sheep have gone astray; we have turned every one to his own way; and the LORD hath laid on him the iniquity of us all" (Isaiah 53:6).

Except for Jesus, every human being who has ever lived has

committed sin. In Romans 6:23, the Bible tells us that "the wages of sin *is* death." Your sin has *earned* you the death penalty. You *deserve* to spend eternity in Hell, because God cannot tolerate even the smallest sin. However Jesus, Who had no sin, "took the rap" for you. In other words, God allowed Jesus to die in your place, so that you wouldn't have to die: "the LORD hath laid on him the iniquity of us all."

Blood is the only thing that can take away sin. The blood that Jesus shed bought you the right to escape the death penalty and choose eternal life. We have a blood covenant with God. Even the Old Covenant—the Old Testament—was a blood covenant. The book of Hebrews tells us:

> Whereupon neither the first testament was dedicated without blood. For when Moses had spoken every precept to all the people according to the law, he took the blood of calves and of goats, with water, and scarlet wool, and hyssop, and sprinkled both the book, and all the people, Saying, This is the blood of the testament which God hath enjoined unto you. Moreover he sprinkled with blood both the tabernacle, and all the vessels of the ministry. And almost all things are by the law purged with blood; and without shedding of blood is no remission.
>
> Hebrews 9:18-22

Old Testament or New, "without shedding of blood is no remission." There is no remission of sins without the shedding of blood. In the Old Testament, God allowed a temporary remission of sins when the blood of animals was shed. On the original Passover, each Jewish household sacrificed a lamb and placed its blood on the door posts so that when God saw the blood He would *pass over* their houses without killing their firstborn.

Then or now, it is blood that saves us from the wrath of God. In First Corinthians 5:7, Paul compared Jesus to the Passover lamb when he said, "For even Christ our passover is sacrificed for us."

John the Baptist called Jesus the Lamb of God. "The next day John seeth Jesus coming unto him, and saith, Behold the Lamb of God, which taketh away the sin of the world" (John 1:29).

Jesus was a man. Why did John call him a lamb? He was the Lamb of God because He had been sent to this world in order to be our Passover Lamb, the Lamb that would be sacrificed for us. He would die for our sins so that we would not have to die for them.

In the same way that lambs were offered upon Old Testament altars to atone for the sins of sinful men, Jesus, the Lamb of God, was to die on the Cross in the place of sinful men.

Jesus ministered to the people, giving us a foretaste of what the ministry of the church should be. And at last the man of Golgotha was crucified in order that the world might know the cleansing power of the blood, and so that the gates of salvation would open wide. "He came unto his own, and his own received him not. But as many as received him, to them gave he power to become the sons of God, even to them that believe on his name" (John 1:11-12).

My friends, I want to emphasize it right now. I would like to burn it into your soul. I want to put it in such language that you will never be able to forget it in the future. Please listen to me: without the Blood of Jesus there is no remission of sin. And even though Jesus died for you—suffered for you—shed His Blood for you—you must receive Him before that Blood will be applied to your life.

"But as many as *received him*, to them gave he power to become the sons of God."

Church membership will not save you.

Good deeds won't save you.

Philanthropy won't save you.

Only Jesus can save you.

# What Salvation Means

Going to church is good, but going to church doesn't make you a Christian any more than going into a garage turns you into a car.

My natural birth was a miracle. I was stillborn: the doctors had given me up for dead. But as my mother lay in the hospital, the Lord spoke to her through a vision and told her, "Fear not, the child will not die, but the child will live. Do not name him Patrick after your father but name him Christos."

Shortly afterward, the doctor decided to make one last try to save my life, and this time it worked. As my father used to tell it, I was lying on the shelf like a brick... "But suddenly Christos began to kick, and he is still kicking today."

But even though I was named after the Lord, even though I had seen Jesus in a vision as a child, I somehow forgot these things. My wife got saved, and I wanted no part of it. For two years, she prayed that God would either save me or take me. God almost took me. One night I was in a serious car accident. I skidded off the highway into a ditch, uprooting a tree. I broke my jaw in four places and my nose in one. I had multiple internal injuries. I knew it was very likely that I might die. I was lonely and in despair. As they rushed me to the hospital, I knew Jesus' name as well as I knew my own name, because I was named after Him. I cried out to Jesus, but I had very little faith that God would hear me. It wasn't until after they got me to the hospital that a light suddenly filled the room. I was filled with a supernatural peace. I felt as though I was being lifted into the air. Then I saw Jesus. He placed His hand on my hand and said, "Chris Panos, I have called you to preach My Bible unto all the world."

When I had my car accident, I realized that I was destined for hell if God didn't intervene. If there is anything that I thank God for, it is that He visited me that night. However, you do not need a visitation from Jesus in order to be saved. You do not need to be a good person. You do not need to be a bad person. All you need to do is to receive Jesus as your Savior, ask Him to forgive your sins, and commit to live your life for Him.

Perhaps you think you can't live up to what Jesus expects of you. That's right—until you're saved, you really can't. You may be bound by drugs or alcohol or sexual addiction or some other form of sin. Even if you think you're a "good person," you're undoubtedly breaking what Jesus said was the most important commandment, which is to love the Lord your God with all your heart, all your soul, all your mind, and all your strength. You can't do that unless Jesus is living in your heart. Do you have Him there? Is Jesus dwelling in your soul? Jesus Christ can still break the power of sin. Jesus Christ can still set the prisoner free! Jesus Christ can and will do whatever it takes to enable you to live for Him, if *you* will ask Him.

There is not a person in the world too hard for God to save. Nothing is impossible with God. I don't care how badly you are bound; I don't care what your past has been, I don't care what other people say about you, if you will give all that you are and all that you hope to be in real surrender before God, something will happen to you. You will be saved. You will be saved because you know the Savior. You will be saved because you received Him. You will be saved because you asked the living Christ to come into your heart.

He will set you free of every habit you yield to Him. Drugs? Alcohol? Sex? Pornography? Addictions can vanish right now if you receive Him.

There is no salvation without the Savior, Jesus Christ. Sometimes we are so absorbed in the adoration of the things He gave us that we have forgotten the One who gave them.

In our teachings we have forgotten the Teacher.

I love what He taught; I reverence what He said; I want to walk in the light of His Word. Don't you? His Word is not a philosophy. It is not a theological document. It is not just a lifestyle. It is Christ in your heart.

Until you are saved, you cannot know God, because the

Bible tells us that "the natural man receiveth not the things of the Spirit of God: for they are foolishness unto him: neither can he know *them*, because they are spiritually discerned" (1 Corinthians 2:14).

Right now, stop. Confess your sins and receive Jesus Christ as your Lord.

The Bible says "That if thou shalt confess with thy mouth the Lord Jesus, and shalt believe in thine heart that God hath raised him from the dead, thou shalt be saved. For with the heart man believeth unto righteousness; and with the mouth confession is made unto salvation. For the scripture saith, Whosoever believeth on him shall not be ashamed" (Romans 10:9-11).

Why not pray this prayer right now?

*Heavenly Father, I know that I am guilty of sin and*
*my sins have separated me from You.*
*I ask You to forgive me for all of my sins and help*
*me to live a life that pleases You.*
*I believe that Jesus Christ died for my sins, shed His*
*blood to cleanse me from sin, was resurrected from*
*the dead, and hears this prayer.*
*I now invite You, Jesus, to become the Lord of my*
*life, to reign in my heart from this day forward.*
*I receive You as my personal Lord and Savior, and*
*confess with my mouth that **Jesus is my Lord**.*
*Amen.*

When you prayed this prayer, please let me know about it so that we may rejoice together. Write to me at Chris Panos, P. 0. Box 3333, Houston, Texas U.S.A. 77253-3333. Or email me at chrispanos@chrispanos.com. And of course you're invited to visit my web site at www.chrispanos.com.

*APPENDICES*

# APPENDIX A

# EMERGENCY SUPPLY LIST FROM THE HOMELAND SECURITY WEB SITE

Through its Ready Campaign, the US Department of Homeland Security educates and empowers Americans to take some simple steps to prepare for and respond to potential emergencies, including natural disasters and terrorist attacks. Ready asks individuals to do three key things: get an emergency supply kit, make a family emergency plan, and be informed about the different types of emergencies that could occur and their appropriate responses.

All Americans should have some basic supplies on hand in order to survive for at least three days if an emergency occurs. Following is a listing of some basic items that every emergency supply kit should include. However, it is important that individuals review this list and consider where they live and the unique needs of their family in order to create an emergency supply kit that will meet these needs. Individuals should also consider having at least two emergency supply kits, one full kit at home and smaller portable kits in their workplace, vehicle or other places they spend time.

U.S. Department of Homeland Security
Washington, DC 20528

## ✓ Recommended Items to Include in a Basic Emergency Supply Kit:

❑ Water, one gallon of water per person per day for at least three days, for drinking and sanitation
❑ Food, at least a three-day supply of non-perishable food
❑ Battery-powered or hand crank radio and a NOAA Weather Radio with tone alert and extra batteries for both
❑ Flashlight and extra batteries
❑ First aid kit [Don't forget potassium iodide pills, in case of fallout—C.P.]
❑ Whistle to signal for help
❑ Dust mask, to help filter contaminated air [An NBC gas mask would be much better—C.P.] and plastic sheeting and duct tape to shelter-in-place
❑ Moist towelettes, garbage bags and plastic ties for personal sanitation
❑ Wrench or pliers to turn off utilities
❑ Can opener for food (if kit contains canned food)
❑ Local maps

## ✓ Additional Items to Consider Adding to an Emergency Supply Kit:

❑ Prescription medications and glasses
❑ Infant formula and diapers
❑ Pet food and extra water for your pet
❑ Important family documents such as copies of insurance policies, identification and bank account records in a waterproof, portable container
❑ Cash or traveler's checks and change

- ❑ Emergency reference material such as a first aid book or information from www.ready.gov
- ❑ Sleeping bag or warm blanket for each person. Consider additional bedding if you live in a cold-weather climate.
- ❑ Complete change of clothing including a long sleeved shirt, long pants and sturdy shoes. Consider additional clothing if you live in a cold-weather climate.
- ❑ Household chlorine bleach and medicine dropper – When diluted nine parts water to one part bleach, bleach can be used as a disinfectant. Or in an emergency, you can use it to treat water by using 16 drops of regular household liquid bleach per gallon of water. Do not use scented, color safe or bleaches with added cleaners.
- ❑ Fire Extinguisher
- ❑ Matches in a waterproof container
- ❑ Feminine supplies and personal hygiene items
- ❑ Mess kits, paper cups, plates and plastic utensils, paper towels
- ❑ Paper and pencil
- ❑ Books, games, puzzles or other activities for children[174]

# APPENDIX B

# FOOD AND WATER IN AN EMERGENCY

*In a disaster, you might be cut off from food, water and electricity for days. By preparing emergency provisions, you can turn what could be a life-threatening situation into a manageable problem.*

Federal Emergency Management Agency                American Red Cross

If an earthquake, hurricane, winter storm or other disaster strikes your community, you might not have access to food, water and electricity for days, or even weeks. By taking some time now to store emergency food and water supplies, you can provide for your entire family. This brochure was developed by the Federal Emergency Management Agency in cooperation with the American Red Cross and the U.S. Department of Agriculture. Having an ample supply of clean water is a top priority in an emerge n cy. A normally active person needs to drink at least two quarts of water each day. Hot environments can double that amount. Children, nursing mothers and ill people will need even more. You will also need water for food prep a ration and hygiene. Store a total of at least one gallon per person, per day. You should store at least a two - week supply of water for each member of your family. If supplies run low, never ration water. Drink the amount you need today, and try to find more for tomorrow. You can minimize the amount of water your body needs by reducing activity and staying cool.

## How to Store Water

Store your water in thoroughly washed plastic, glass, fiberglass or enamel-lined metal containers. Never use a container that has held toxic substances. Plastic containers, such as soft drink bottles, are best. You can also purchase food-grade plastic buckets or drums. Seal water containers tightly, label them and store in a cool, dark place. Rotate water every six months.

## Emergency Outdoor Water Sources

If you need to find water outside your home, you can use these sources. Be sure to purify the water according to the instructions on page 3 before drinking it.
- Rainwater
- Streams, rivers and other moving bodies of water
- Ponds and lakes
- Natural springs

Avoid water with floating material, an odor or dark color. Use saltwater only if you distill it first. You should not drink flood water.

## Food Supplies

### Short-Term Food Supplies

Even though it is unlikely that an emergency would cut off your food supply for two weeks, you should prepare a supply that will last that long.

The easiest way to develop a two-week stockpile is to

increase the amount of basic foods you normally keep on your shelves.

## Storage Tips

- Keep food in a dry, cool spot—a dark area if possible.
- Keep food covered at all times.
- Open food boxes or cans carefully so that you can close them tightly after each use.
- Wrap cookies and crackers in plastic bags, and keep them in tight containers.
- Empty opened packages of sugar, dried fruits and nuts into screw-top jars or air-tight cans to protect them from pests.
- Inspect all food for signs of spoilage before use.
- Use foods before they go bad, and replace them with fresh supplies, dated with ink or marker. Place new items at the back of the storage area and older ones in front.

## Nutrition Tips

- During and right after a disaster, it will be vital that you maintain your strength. So remember:
- Eat at least one well-balanced meal each day.
- Drink enough liquid to enable your body to function properly (two quarts a day).
- Take in enough calories to enable you to do any necessary work.
- Include vitamin, mineral and protein supplements in your stockpile to assure adequate nutrition.

# Hidden Water Sources in Your Home

If a disaster catches you without a stored supply of clean water, you can use the water in your hot-water tank, pipes and ice cubes. As a last resort, you can use water in the reservoir tank of your toilet (not the bowl).

Do you know the location of your incoming water valve?

You'll need to shut it off to stop contaminated water from entering your home if you hear reports of broken water or sewage lines.

To use the water in your pipes, let air into the plumbing by turning on the faucet in your house at the highest level. A small amount of water will trickle out. Then obtain water from the lowest faucet in the house.

To use the water in your hot-water tank, be sure the electricity or gas is off, and open the drain at the bottom of the tank. Start the water flowing by turning off the water intake valve and turning on a hot-water faucet. Do not turn on the gas or electricity when the tank is empty.

## When Food Supplies Are Low

If activity is reduced, healthy people can survive on half their usual food intake for an extended period and without any food for many days. Food, unlike water, may be rationed safely, except for children and pregnant women.

If your water supply is limited, try to avoid foods that are high in fat and protein, and don't stock salty foods, since they will make you thirsty. Try to eat salt-free crackers, whole grain cereals and canned foods with high liquid content.

You don't need to go out and buy unfamiliar foods to prepare an emergency food supply. You can use the canned foods, dry mixes and other staples on your cupboard shelves. In fact, familiar foods are important. They can lift morale and give a feeling of security in time of stress. Also, canned foods won't require cooking, water or special preparation. Following are recommended short-term food storage plans.

## Special Considerations

As you stock food, take into account your family's unique needs and tastes. Try to include foods that they will enjoy and that are also high in calories and nutrition. Foods that require no refrigeration, preparation or cooking are best.

Individuals with special diets and allergies will need particular attention, as will babies, toddlers and elderly people. Nursing mothers may need liquid formula, in case they are unable to nurse. Canned dietetic foods, juices and soups may be helpful for ill or elderly people.

Make sure you have a manual can opener and disposable utensils. And don't forget nonperishable foods for your pets.

## How to Cook If the Power Goes Out

For emergency cooking you can use a fireplace, or a charcoal grill or camp stove can be used outdoors. You can also heat food with candle warmers, chafing dishes and fondue pots. Canned food can be eaten right out of the can. If you heat it in the can, be sure to open the can and remove the label first

## Three Ways to Purify Water

In addition to having a bad odor and taste, contaminated water can contain microorganisms that cause diseases such as dysentery, typhoid and hepatitis. You should purify all water of uncertain purity before using it for drinking, food preparation or hygiene.

There are many ways to purify water. None is perfect. Often the best solution is a combination of methods.

Two easy purification methods are outlined below. These measures will kill most microbes but will not remove other contaminants such as heavy metals, salts and most other chemicals. Before purifying, let any suspended particles settle to the bottom, or strain them through layers of paper towel or clean cloth.

**BOILING.** Boiling is the safest method of purifying water. Bring water to a rolling boil for 3-5 minutes, keeping in mind that some water will evaporate. Let the water cool before drinking.

Boiled water will taste better if you put oxygen back into it by pouring the water back and forth between two clean containers. This will also improve the taste of stored water.

**DISINFECTION**. You can use household liquid bleach to kill microorganisms. Use only regular household liquid bleach that contains 5.25 percent sodium hypochlorite. Do not use scented bleaches, colorsafe bleaches or bleaches with added cleaners.

Add 16 drops of bleach per gallon of water, stir and let stand for 30 minutes. If the water does not have a slight bleach odor, repeat the dosage and let stand another 15 minutes.

The only agent used to purify water should be household liquid bleach. Other chemicals, such as iodine or water treatment products sold in camping or surplus stores that do not contain 5.25 percent sodium hypochlorite as the only active ingredient, are not recommended and should not be used.

While the two methods described above will kill most microbes in water, distillation will remove microbes that resist these methods, and heavy metals, salts and most other chemicals.

**DISTILLATION**. Distillation involves boiling water and then collecting the vapor that condenses back to water. The condensed vapor will not include salt and other impurities. To distill, fill a pot halfway with water. Tie a cup to the handle on the pot's lid so that the cup will hang right-side-up when the lid is upside-down (make sure the cup is not dangling into the water) and boil the water for 20 minutes. The water that drips from the lid into the cup is distilled.

## Shelf-life of Foods for Storage

Here are some general guidelines for rotating common emergency foods.
- Use within six months:
  — Powdered milk *(boxed)*
  — Dried fruit *(in metal container)*
  — Dry, crisp crackers *(in metal container)*
  — Potatoes
- Use within one year:

— Canned condensed meat and vegetable soups
— Canned fruits, fruit juices and vegetables
— Ready-to-eat cereals and uncooked instant cereals (in metal containers)
— Peanut butter
— Jelly
— Hard candy and canned nuts
— Vitamin C
• May be stored indefinitely (in proper containers and conditions):
— Wheat
— Vegetable oils
— Dried corn
— Baking powder
— Soybeans
— Instant coffee, tea and cocoa
— Salt
— Noncarbonated soft drinks
— White rice
— Bouillon products
— Dry pasta
— Powdered milk (in nitrogen-packed cans)

# Disaster Supplies

## Supplies

It's 2:00 a.m. and a flash flood forces you to evacuate your home—fast. There's no time to gather food from the kitchen, fill bottles with water, grab a first-aid kit from the closet and snatch a flashlight and a portable radio from the bedroom. You need to have these items packed and ready in one place before disaster strikes.

Pack at least a three-day supply of food and water, and store it in a handy place. Choose foods that are easy to carry, nutritious and ready-to-eat. In addition, pack these emergency items:
• Medical supplies and first aid manual

- Hygiene supplies
- Portable radio, flashlights and extra batteries
- Shovel and other useful tools
- Household liquid bleach to purify drinking water.
- Money and matches in a waterproof container
- Fire extinguisher
- Blanket and extra clothing
- Infant and small children's needs (*if appropriate*)
- Manual can opener

## If the Electricity Goes Off . . .

FIRST, use perishable food and foods from the refrigerator.

THEN, use the foods from the freezer. To minimize the number of times you open the freezer door, post a list of freezer contents on it. In a well-filled, well-insulated freezer, foods will usually still have ice crystals in their centers (meaning foods are safe to eat) for at least three days.

FINALLY, begin to use non-perishable foods and staples.

Learn More

If you are interested in learning more about how to prepare for emergencies, contact your local or State Office of Emergency Management or local American Red Cross chapter, or write to

> FEMA
> PO BOX 2012
> JESSUP MD 20794-2012
>
> And ask for any of the following publications:
> Emergency Preparedness Checklist
> (L-154) Item #8-0872 ARC 4463
>
> Your Family Disaster Supplies Kit
> (L-189) Item #8-0941 ARC 4463

Your Family Disaster Supplies Kit
(L-191) Item #8-0941 ARC 4463

Your Family Disaster Plan
(L-191) Item #8-0954 ARC 4466

Are You Ready? Your Guide to Disaster Preparedness
(H-34) Item #8-0908

Emergency Preparedness Publications
(L-164) Item #8-0822[175]

# APPENDIX C

# RESPONDING TO A BIOLOGICAL OR CHEMICAL THREAT: A PRACTICAL GUIDE[176]

## Released by the Bureau of Diplomatic Security November 2001

### Introduction

This pamphlet provides a broad overview of the chemical and biological terrorist threat and, drawing on the lessons learned from the few chemical and biological incidents to date, suggests some basic means of detection, defense, and decontamination. The intention is not to alarm people but to enable employees and their family members to recognize and properly react to a chemical or biological situation in the event they encounter one.

In 1995, the Aum Shinrikyo, a Japanese religious cult now known as Aleph, launched a large-scale chemical attack on the Tokyo subway system. The attack focused on four stations using Sarin gas, a potent chemical warfare nerve agent. Twelve people were killed but the attack fell far short of the apparent objective to inflict thousands of casualties. Subsequent investigation by authorities revealed that the cult had previously conducted several unsuccessful attacks against a variety of targets using other chemical agents and the biological agents botulism toxin and anthrax.

Since 1997, religious organizations, health clinics, and Government agencies in Indiana, Kentucky, Tennessee, California, Hawaii, and the District of Columbia, among other states, have received threatening letters purporting to contain the biological agent anthrax. While none of the letters were found to contain anthrax, they caused considerable fear and disruption where received.

Disturbing as they are, these incidents serve to illustrate a potentially new type of terrorist threat of concern to law enforcement and emergency planning officials throughout the U.S. Government. The State Department and its Diplomatic Security Service share that concern and have taken, and will continue to take, appropriate steps to meet the potential consequences of this threat.

If you or your family members require additional details about this or any security-related subject, please contact the regional security officer (RSO) at your post of assignment.

Aside from their common lethality, there is no "one size fits all" when it comes to describing the types and effects of possible chemical or biological agents. Chemical agents are generally liquids, often aerosolized, and most have immediate effects or are delayed for a few hours. Many chemical agents have a unique odor and color. Biological agents differ in that the effects are delayed, often for days. The effects of toxins, such as botulinum toxin, occur typically in less than a day. Living biological agents, such as anthrax or plague, generally take 2-5 days for symptoms to appear. Biological agents have no odor or color and can be in either liquid or powder form. There are many different potential chemical and biological agents that a terrorist could use as a weapon, but we can make the following broad generalizations:

- Although food or water contamination or absorption through the skin are possible attack routes, most experts agree that inhalation of chemical or biological agents is the most likely and effective means. Protection of breathing airways is therefore the single most important factor in a situation where chemical or biological agents may be present.
- Many likely agents are heavier than air and would tend to stay close to the ground. This dictates an upward safehaven strategy.
- Basic decontamination procedures are generally the same no matter what the agent. Thorough scrubbing with large amounts of warm soapy water or a mixture of 10 parts water to 1 part bleach (10:1) will greatly reduce the possibility of absorbing an agent through the skin.
- If water is not available, talcum powder or flour are also excellent means of decontamination of liquid agents. Sprinkle the flour or powder liberally over the affected skin area, wait 30 seconds, and brush off with a rag or gauze pad. (Note: The powder absorbs the agent so it must be brushed off thoroughly. If available, rubber gloves should be used when carrying out this procedure.)
- Generally, chemical agents tend to present an immediately noticeable effect, whereas many biological agents will take days before symptoms appear. In either case, medical attention should be sought immediately, even if exposure is thought to be limited.
- Most chemical and biological agents that present an inhalation hazard will break down fairly rapidly when exposed to the sun, diluted with water, or dissipated in high winds.
- No matter what the agent or its concentration, evacuation from the area of attack is always advisable unless you are properly equipped with an appropriate breathing device and protective clothing or have access to collective protection.

## Warning Signs of An Attack or Incident

A chemical or biological attack or incident won't always be immediately apparent given the fact that many agents are odorless and colorless and some cause no immediately noticeable effects or symptoms. Be alert to the possible presence of agent. Indicators of such an attack include:

- Droplets of oily film on surfaces
- Unusual dead or dying animals in the area
- Unusual liquid sprays or vapors
- Unexplained odors (smell of bitter almonds, peach kernels, newly mown hay, or green grass)
- Unusual or unauthorized spraying in the area
- Victims displaying symptoms of nausea, difficulty breathing, convulsions, disorientation, or patterns of illness inconsistent with natural disease
- Low-lying clouds or fog unrelated to weather; clouds of dust; or suspended, possibly colored, particles
- People dressed unusually (long-sleeved shirts or overcoats in the summertime) or wearing breathing protection particularly in areas where large numbers of people tend to congregate, such as subways or stadiums

## What To Do In Case of Attack

Protection of breathing airways is the single most important thing a person can do in the event of a chemical or biological incident or attack. In most cases, absent a handy gas mask, the only sure way to protect an airway is to put distance between you and the source of the agent. While evacuating the area, cover your mouth and nose with a handkerchief, coat sleeve, or any piece of cloth to provide some moderate means of protection. Other basic steps one can take to avoid or mitigate exposure to chemical or biological agents include:

- Stay alert for attack warning signs. Early detection enhances survival.

- Move upwind from the source of the attack.
- If evacuation from the immediate area is impossible, move indoors (if outside) and upward to an interior room on a higher floor. Remember many agents are heavier than air and will tend to stay close to the ground.
- Once indoors, close all windows and exterior doors and shut down air conditioning or heating systems to prevent circulation of air.
- Cover your mouth and nose. If gas masks are not available, use a surgical mask or a handkerchief. An improvised mask can be made by soaking a clean cloth in a solution of 1 tablespoon of baking soda in a cup of water. While this is not highly effective, it may provide some protection. Cover bare arms and legs and make sure any cuts or abrasions are covered or bandaged.
- If splashed with an agent, immediately wash it off using copious amounts of warm soapy water or a diluted 10:1 bleach solution.
- Letters from unknown sources should first be screened by security personnel. If opened, letters allegedly containing anthrax or another toxin should be handled carefully. Note if there was a puff of dust or particles from the envelope when it was opened and be sure to report that when assistance arrives. Carefully place such a letter and its envelope in a sealed plastic pouch. Thoroughly wash face and hands with warm soapy water before calling for assistance.
- If circumstances dictate, plan and prepare a chemical/biological safehaven in your residence using guidelines listed in this pamphlet.
- At the office, familiarize yourself in advance with established emergency procedures and equipment at your post. See your regional or post security officer for details.
- If in a car, shut off outside air intake vents and roll up windows if no gas has entered the vehicle. Late model cars may provide some protection from toxic agents.
- In any case of suspected exposure to chemical or biological

agents, no matter what the origin, medical assistance should be sought as soon as possible, even if no symptoms are immediately evident.

## Preparing a Safehaven

In some remote but possible scenarios (such as the incident in Bhopal, India) an entire city or neighborhood could become endangered by lethal gas. If conditions at your post make this a possibility, you may want to plan and prepare a sealed chemical/biological safehaven at your residence as follows:

## Choosing a Safehaven Room

- Select an inner room on an upstairs floor with the least number of windows and doors.
- Choose a large room with access to a bathroom and preferably with a telephone.
- Avoid choosing rooms with window or wall air conditioners; they are more difficult to seal.

## Sealing a Room

- Close all windows, doors, and shutters.
- Seal all cracks around window and door frames with wide tape.
- Cover windows and exterior doors with plastic sheets (6 mil minimum) and seal with pressure-sensitive adhesive tape. (This provides a second barrier should the window break or leak.)
- Seal all openings in windows and doors (including keyholes) and any cracks with cotton wool or wet rags and duct tape. A water-soaked cloth should be used to seal gaps under doors.
- Shut down all window and central air and heating units.

## Suggested Safehaven Equipment

- Protective equipment--biological/chemical rated gas masks, if available; waterproof clothing including long-sleeved shirts, long pants, raincoats, boots, and rubber gloves.

- Food and water--a 3-day supply.
- Emergency equipment--flashlights, battery-operated radio, extra batteries, can or bottle opener, knife and scissors, first aid kit, fire extinguisher, etc.
- Miscellaneous items--prescription medicines and eyeglasses, fan, extra blankets, passports and other important papers, television set, toys, books, and games.

# APPENDIX D

# ANNUAL THREAT ASSESSMENT OF THE DIRECTOR OF NATIONAL INTELLIGENCE FOR THE SENATE SELECT COMMITTEE ON INTELLIGENCE

## February 2, 2006

## John D. Negroponte

## Director of National Intelligence

# Statement by the Director of National Intelligence, John D. Negroponte to the Senate Select Committee On Intelligence 2 February 2006[177]

Chairman Roberts, Vice-Chairman Rockefeller, Members of the Committee, thank you for the invitation to offer my assessment of the threats, challenges, and opportunities for the United States in today's world.

I am honored to be the first Director of National Intelligence to offer you such an assessment, and am pleased to note that following my oral testimony, I will answer your questions with the assistance of: Mr. Porter Goss, Director of the Central Intelligence Agency; Lieutenant General Michael D. Maples, Director of the Defense Intelligence Agency; Mr. Robert Mueller, Director of the Federal Bureau of Investigation; Ms. Carol Rodley, Acting Assistant Secretary of State for Intelligence and Research; Mr. Charles E. Allen, Chief Intelligence Officer, Department of Homeland Security; and General Michael Hayden, Principal Deputy Director of National Intelligence.

Let me begin with a straightforward statement of preoccupation shared by all of us sitting here before you: terrorism is the preeminent threat to our citizens, Homeland, interests, and friends. The War on Terror is our first priority and driving concern as we press ahead with a major transformation of the Intelligence Community we represent.

We live in a world that is full of conflict, contradictions, and accelerating change. Viewed from the perspective of the Director of National Intelligence, the most dramatic change of all is the exponential increase in the number of targets we must identify, track, and analyze. Today, in addition to hostile nation-states, we are focusing on terrorist groups, proliferation networks, alienated communities, charismatic individuals, narcotraffickers, and microscopic influenza.

The 21$^{st}$ century is less dangerous than the 20$^{th}$ century in certain respects, but more dangerous in others. Globalization, particularly of technologies that can be used to produce WMD, political instability around the world, the rise of emerging powers like China, the spread of the jihadist movement, and of course, the horrific events of September 11, 2001, demand heightened vigilance from our Intelligence Community.

This morning, then, I will discuss:

- Global jihadists, their fanatical ideology, and the civilized world's efforts to disrupt, dismantle and destroy their networks;
- The struggle of the Iraqi and Afghan people to assert their sovereignty over insurgency, terror, and extremism;
- WMD-related proliferation and two states of particular concern, Iran and North Korea;
- Issues of political instability and governance in all regions of the world that affect our ability to protect and advance our interests; and
- Globalization, emerging powers, and such transnational challenges as the geopolitics of energy, narcotrafficking, and possible pandemics.

In assessing these themes, we all must be mindful of the old dictum: forewarned is forearmed. Our policymakers, warfighters, and law enforcement officers need the best intelligence and analytic insight humanly and technically possible to help them peer into the onrushing shadow of the future and make the decisions that will protect American lives and interests. This has never been more true than now with US and Coalition forces in Iraq and Afghanistan— and the citizens and fledgling governments they help to protect— under attack. Addressing threats to their safety and providing the critical intelligence on a myriad of tactical and strategic issues must be—and is —a top priority for our Intelligence Community.

But in discussing all the many dangers the 21$^{st}$ century poses, it should be emphasized that they do not befall America alone. The issues we consider today confront responsible leaders everywhere. That is the true nature of the 21st century: accelerating change affecting and challenging us all.

## THE GLOBAL JIHADIST THREAT

Collaboration with our friends and allies around the world has helped us achieve some notable successes against the global jihadist threat. In fact, most of al-Qa'ida's setbacks last year were the result of our allies' efforts, either independently or with our assistance. And since 9/11, examples of the high level of counterterrorism efforts around the world are many. Pakistan's commitment has enabled some of the most important captures to date. Saudi Arabia's resolve to counter the spread of terrorism has increased. Our relationship with Spain has strengthened since the March 2004 Madrid train bombings. The British have long been our closest counterterrorism partners—the seamless cooperation in the aftermath of the July attacks in London reflected that commitment—while Australia, Canada, France and many other nations remain stout allies. Nonetheless, much remains to be done; the battle is far from over.

Jihadists seek to overthrow regimes they regard as "apostate" and to eliminate US influence in the Muslim world. They attack Americans when they can, but most of their targets and victims are fellow Muslims. Nonetheless, the slow pace of economic, social, and political change in most Muslim majority nations continues to fuel a global jihadist movement. The movement is diffuse and subsumes three quite different types of groups and individuals:

- First and foremost, al Qa'ida, a battered but resourceful organization;

- Second, other Sunni jihadist groups, some affiliated with al-Qa'ida, some not;

- Third, networks and cells that are the self-generating

progeny of al-Qa'ida.

- **Al-Qa'ida Remains Our Top Concern.** We have eliminated much of the leadership that presided over al-Qa'ida in 2001, and US-led counterterrorism efforts in 2005 continue to disrupt its operations, take out its leaders and deplete it s cadre. But the organization's core elements still plot and make preparations for terrorist strikes against the Homeland and other targets from bases in the Pakistan-Afghanistan border area; they also have gained added reach through their merger with the Iraq-based network of Abu Mus'ab al-Zarqawi, which has broadened al-Qa'ida's appeal within the jihadist community and potentially put new resources at its disposal.

Thanks to effective intelligence operations, we know a great deal about al Qa'ida's vision. Zawahiri, al Qa'ida's number two, is candid in his July 2005 letter to Zarqawi. He portrays the jihad in Iraq as a stepping-stone in the march toward a global caliphate, with the focus on Egypt, Syria, Jordan, Lebanon, Saudi Arabia, the Gulf states, and Israel. Zawahiri stresses the importance of having a secure base in Iraq from which to launch attacks elsewhere, including in the US Homeland.

In Bin Laden's recent audio tape, al- Qa'ida's top leader reaffirms the group's commitment to attack our Homeland and attempts to reassure supporters by claiming that the reason there has been no attack on the US since 2001 is that he chose not to do so. This week's statement by Zawahiri is another indication that the group's leadership is not completely cutoff and can continue to get its message out to followers. The quick turnaround time and the frequency of Zawahiri statements in the past year underscore the high priority al-Qa'ida places on propaganda from its most senior leaders.

Attacking the US Homeland, US interests overseas, and US allies—in that order—are al-Qa'ida's top operational priorities. The group will attempt high-impact attacks for as long as its central command structure is functioning and affiliated groups are capable of furthering its interests, because even modest operational capabilities can yield a deadly and damaging attack. Although an attack using conventional explosives continues to be the most probable scenario, al-Qa'ida remains interested in acquiring chemical, biological, radiological, and nuclear materials or weapons to attack the United States, US troops, and US interests worldwide.

Indeed, today, we are more likely to see an attack from terrorists using weapons or agents of mass destruction than states, although terrorists' capabilities would be much more limited. In fact, intelligence reporting indicates that nearly 40 terrorist organizations, insurgencies, or cults have used, possessed, or expressed an interest in chemical, biological, radiological, or nuclear agents or weapons. Many are capable of conducting simple, small-scale attacks, such as poisonings, or using improvised chemical devices.

**Al-Qa'ida Inspires Other Sunni Jihadists.** The global jihadist movement also subsumes other Sunni extremist organizations, allied with or inspired by al-Qa'ida's global anti-Western agenda. These groups pose less danger to the US Homeland than does al-Qa'ida, but they increasingly threaten our allies and interests abroad and are working to expand their reach and capabilities to conduct multiple and/or mass-casualty attacks outside their traditional areas of operation.

**Jemaah Islamiya (JI)** is a well-organized group responsible for dozens of attacks killing hundreds of people in Southeast Asia. The threat of a JI attack against US interests is greatest in Southeast Asia, but we assess that the group is committed to helping al-Qa'ida with attacks outside the region.

The **Islamic Jihad Union (IJU),** which has allied itself with al-Qa'ida, operates in Central Asia and was responsible for the July 2004 attacks against the US and Israeli Embassies in Uzbekistan.

The **Libyan Islamic Fighting Group (LIFG)** was formed to establish an Islamic state in Libya, but since the late 1990s it has expanded its goals to include anti-Western jihad alongside al-

Qa'ida. LIFG has called on Muslims everywhere to fight the US In Iraq.

**Pakistani militant groups**—primarily focused on the Kashmir conflict— represent a persistent threat to regional stability and US interests in South Asia and the Near East. They also pose a potential threat to our interests worldwide. Extremists convicted in Virginia in 2003 of providing material support to terrorism trained with a Pakistani group, Lashkar-i-Tayyiba, before 9/11.

**New Jihadist Networks and Cells.** An important part of al-Qa'ida's strategy is to encourage a grassroots uprising of Muslims against the West. Emerging new networks and cells—the third element of the global jihadist threat—reflect aggressive jihadist efforts to exploit feelings of frustration and powerlessness in some Muslim communities, and to fuel the perception that the US is anti-Islamic. Their rationale for using terrorism against the US and establishing strict Islamic practices resonates with a small subset of Muslims. This has led to the emergence of a decentralized and diffused movement, with minimal centralized guidance or control and numerous individuals and small cells—like those who conducted the May 2003 bombing in Morocco, the March 2004 bombings in Spain, and the July 2005 bombings in the UK. Members of these groups have drawn inspiration from al-Qa'ida but appear to operate on their own.

Such unaffiliated individuals, groups and cells represent a different threat than that of a defined organization. They are harder to spot and represent a serious intelligence challenge.

Regrettably, we are not immune from the threat of such "homegrown" jihadist cells. A network of Islamic extremists in Lodi, California, for example, maintained connections with Pakistani militant groups, recruited US citizens for training at radical Karachi madrassas, sponsored Pakistani citizens for travel to the US to work at mosques and madrassas, and according to FBI information, allegedly raised funds for international jihadist groups. In addition, prisons continue to be fertile recruitment ground for extremists who try to exploit converts to Islam.

**Impact of Iraq on Global Jihad.** Should the Iraqi people prevail in establishing a stable political and security environment, the jihadists will be perceived to have failed and fewer jihadists will leave Iraq determined to carry on the fight elsewhere. But, we assess that should the jihadists thwart the Iraqis' efforts to establish a stable political and security environment, they could secure an operational base in Iraq and inspire sympathizers elsewhere to move beyond rhetoric to attempt attacks against neighboring Middle Eastern nations, Europe, and even the United States. The same dynamic pertains to al-Zarqawi. His capture would deprive the movement of a notorious leader, whereas his continued acts of terror could enable him to expand his following beyond his organization in Iraq much as Bin Ladin expanded al-Qa'ida in the 1990s.[178]

**Impact of the Islamic Debate.** The debate between Muslim extremists and moderates also will influence the future terrorist environment, the domestic stability of key US partners, and the foreign policies of governments throughout the Muslim world. The violent actions of global jihadists are adding urgency to the debate within Islam over how religion should shape government. Growing internal demands for reform in many Muslim countries further stimulate this debate. In general, Muslims are becoming more aware of their Islamic identity, leading to growing political activism; but this does *not* necessarily signal a trend toward radicalization. Most Muslims reject the extremist message and violent agendas of the global jihadists. Indeed, as Muslims endorse democratic principles of freedom, equality, and the rule of law *and* a role for their religious beliefs in building better futures for their communities, there will be growing opportunities for countering a jihadist movement that only promises more authoritarianism, isolation, and economic stagnation.

# EXTREMISM AND CHALLENGES TO EFFECTIVE GOVERNANCE AND LEGITIMACY IN IRAQ AND AFGHANISTAN

The threat from extremism and anti-Western militancy is especially acute in Iraq and Afghanistan.

In discussing Iraq, I'd like to offer a "balance sheet" to give a sense of where I see things today and what I see as the trends in 2006. Bold, inclusive leadership will be *the* critical factor in establishing an Iraqi constitutional democracy that is both viable as a nation-state and responsive to the diversity of Iraq's regions and people.

Let me begin with some of these encouraging developments before turning to the challenges:

- The insurgents have not been able to establish any lasting territorial control; were unable to disrupt either of the two national elections held this year or the Constitutional referendum; have not developed a political strategy to attract popular support beyond their Sunni Arab base; and have not shown the ability to coordinate nationwide operations.

- Iraqi security forces are taking on more demanding missions, making incremental progress toward operational independence, and becoming more capable of providing the kind of stability Iraqis deserve and the economy needs in order to grow.

- Signs of open conflict between extreme Sunni jihadists and Sunni nationalist elements of the insurgency, while so far still localized, are encouraging and exploitable. The jihadists' heavy-handed activities in Sunni areas in western Iraq have caused tribal and nationalist elements in the insurgency to reach out to the Baghdad government for support.

- Large-scale Sunni participation in the last elections has provided a first step toward diminishing Sunni support for the insurgency. There appears to be a strong desire among Sunnis to explore the potential benefits of political participation.

But numerous challenges remain.

### The Insurgency and Iraqi Security Forces

Iraqi Sunni Arab disaffection is the primary enabler of the insurgency and is likely to remain high in 2006. Even if a broad, inclusive national government emerges, there almost certainly will be a lag time before we see a dampening effect on the insurgency. Insurgents continue to demonstrate the ability to recruit, supply, and attack Coalition and Iraqi Security Forces, and their leaders continue to exploit Islamic themes, nationalism, and personal grievances to fuel opposition to the government and to recruit more fighters.

The most extreme Sunni jihadists, such as those fighting with Zarqawi, will remain unreconciled and continue to attack Iraqis and Coalition forces. These extreme Sunni jihadist elements, a subset of which are foreign fighters, constitute a small minority of the overall insurgency, but their use of high-profile suicide attacks gives them a disproportionate impact. The insurgents' use of increasingly lethal improvised explosive devices (IEDs), and the IED makers' adaptiveness to Coalition countermeasures, remain the most significant day-to-day threat to Coalition forces, and a complex challenge for the Intelligence Community.

Iraqi Security Forces require better command and control mechanisms to improve their effectiveness and are experiencing difficulty in managing ethnic and sectarian divides among their units and personnel.

### Sunni Political Participation

A key to establishing effective governance and security over the next three to five years is enhanced Sunni Arab political participation and a growing perception among Sunnis that the political process is addressing their interests. Sunnis will be focused on obtaining what they consider their demographically appropriate share of leadership positions in the new government—especially on the Constitutional Review Commission. Debates over federalism, central versus local control, and division of resources are likely to be complex. Success in satisfactorily resolving them will be key to advancing stability and prospects for a unified country. Although the Kurds and Shia have been accommodating to the underrepresented Sunnis in 2005, their desire to protect core interests—such as regional autonomy and de-Ba'thification—could make further compromise more difficult.

In the aftermath of the December elections, virtually all of the Iraq parties are seeking to create a broad-based government, but all want it to be formed on their terms. The Shia and the Kurds will be the foundation of any governing coalition, but it is not yet clear to us whether they will include the main Sunni factions, particularly the Iraqi Consensus Front, or other smaller and politically weaker secular groups, such as Ayad Allawi's Iraqi National

List. The Sunni parties have significant expectations for concessions from the Shia and Kurds in order to justify their participation and avoid provoking more insurgent violence directed against Sunni political leaders.

**Governance and Reconstruction**

During the coming year, Iraq's newly elected leadership will face a daunting set of governance tasks. The creation of a new, permanent government and the review of the Constitution by early summer will offer opportunities to find common ground and improve the effectiveness and legitimacy of the central government. There is a danger, however, that political negotiations and dealmaking will prove divisive. This could obstruct efforts to improve government performance, extend Baghdad's reach throughout the country, and build confidence in the democratic political process.

Let me focus on one of those tasks—the economy. Restoration of basic services and the creation of jobs are critical to the well-being of Iraqi citizens, the legitimacy of the new government, and, indirectly, to eroding support for the insurgency. At this point, prospects for economic development in 2006 are constrained by the unstable security situation, insufficient commitment to economic reform, and corruption. Iraq is dependent on oil revenues to fund the government, so insurgents continue to disrupt oil infrastructure, despite the fielding of new Iraqi forces to protect it. Insurgents also are targeting trade and transportation. Intelligence has a key role to play in combating threats to pipelines, electric power grids, and personal safety.

## Afghanistan

Like Iraq, Afghanistan is a fragile new democracy struggling to overcome deep-seated social divisions, decades of repression, and acts of terrorism directed against ordinary citizens, officials, foreign aid workers, and Coalition forces. These and other threats to the Karzai government also threaten important American interests—ranging from the defeat of terrorists who find haven along the Afghanistan-Pakistan border to the suppression of opium production.

Afghan leaders face four critical challenges: containing the insurgency, building central government capacity and extending its authority, further containing warlordism, and confronting pervasive drug criminality.

Intelligence is needed to assist, monitor, and protect Afghan, Coalition, and NATO efforts in all four endeavors.

The volume and geographic scope of attacks increased last year, but the Taliban and other militants have not been able to stop the democratic process or expand their support base beyond Pashtun areas of the south and east. Nevertheless, the insurgent threat will impede the expansion of Kabul's writ, slow economic development, and limit progress in counternarcotics efforts.

Ultimately, defeating the insurgency will depend heavily on continued international aid; effective Coalition, NATO, and Afghan government security operations to prevent the insurgency from gaining a stronger foothold in some Pashtun areas; and the success of the government's reconciliation initiatives.

## WEAPONS OF MASS DESTRUCTION AND STATES OF KEY CONCERN: IRAN AND NORTH KOREA

The ongoing development of dangerous weapons and delivery systems constitutes the second major threat to the safety of our nation, our deployed troops, and our allies. We are most concerned about the threat and destabilizing effect of nuclear proliferation. We are also concerned about the threat from biological agents—or even chemical agents, which would have psychological and possibly political effects far greater than their actual magnitude. Use by nation-states can still be constrained by the logic of deterrence and international control regimes, but these constraints may be of little utility in preventing the use of mass effect weapons by rogue regimes or terrorist groups.

The time when a few states had monopolies over the most dangerous technologies has been over for many years. Moreover, our adversaries have more access to acquire and more opportunities to deliver such weapons than in the past. Technologies, often dual-use, move freely in our globalized economy, as do the scientific personnel who design them. So it is more difficult for us to track efforts to acquire those components and production technologies that are so widely available. The potential dangers of proliferation are so grave that we must do everything possible to discover and disrupt attempts by those who seek to acquire materials and weapons.

We assess that some of the countries that are still pursuing WMD programs will continue to try to improve their capabilities and level of self-sufficiency over the next decade. We also are focused on the potential acquisition of such nuclear, chemical, and/or biological weapons—or the production technologies and materials necessary to produce them—by states that do not now have such programs, terrorist organizations like al-Qa'ida and by criminal organizations, alone or via middlemen.

We are working with other elements of the US Government regarding the safety and security of nuclear weapons and fissile material, pathogens, and chemical weapons in select countries.

**Iran and North Korea: States of Highest Concern**

Our concerns about Iran are shared by many nations, by the IAEA, and of course, Iran's neighbors.

Iran conducted a clandestine uranium enrichment program for nearly two decades in violation of its IAEA safeguards agreement, and despite its claims to the contrary, we assess that Iran seeks nuclear weapons. We judge that Tehran probably does not yet have a nuclear weapon and probably has not yet produced or acquired the necessary fissile material. Nevertheless, the danger that it will acquire a nuclear weapon and the ability to integrate it with the ballistic missiles Iran already possesses is a reason for immediate concern. Iran already has the largest inventory of ballistic missiles in the Middle East, and Tehran views its ballistic missiles as an integral part of its strategy to deter—and if necessary retaliate against—forces in the region, including US forces.

As you are aware, Iran is located at the center of a vital— and volatile— region, has strained relations with its neighbors, and is hostile to the United States, our friends, and our values. President Ahmadi-Nejad has made numerous unacceptable statements since his election, hard-liners have control of all the major branches and institutions of government, and the government has become more effective and efficient at repressing the nascent shoots of personal freedom that had emerged in the late 1990s and earlier in the decade.

Indeed, the regime today is more confident and assertive

than it has been since the early days of the Islamic Republic. Several factors work in favor of the clerical regime's continued hold on power. Record oil and other revenue is permitting generous public spending, fueling strong economic growth, and swelling financial reserves. At the same time, Iran is diversifying its foreign trading partners. Asia's share of Iran's trade has jumped to nearly match Europe's 40-percent share. Tehran sees diversification as a buffer against external efforts to isolate it.

Although regime-threatening instability is unlikely, ingredients for political volatility remain, and Iran is wary of the political progress occurring in neighboring Iraq and Afghanistan. Ahmadi-Nejad's rhetorical recklessness and his inexperience on the national and international stage also increase the risk of a misstep that could spur popular opposition, especially if more experienced conservatives cannot rein in his excesses. Over time, Ahmadi-Nejad's populist economic policies could—if enacted—deplete the government's financial resources and weaken a structurally flawed economy. For now, however, Supreme Leader Khamenei is keeping conservative fissures in check by balancing the various factions in government.

Iranian policy toward Iraq and its activities there represent a particular concern. Iran seeks a Shia-dominated and unified Iraq but also wants the US to experience continued setbacks in our efforts to promote democracy and stability. Accordingly, Iran provides guidance and training to select Iraqi Shia political groups and weapons and training to Shia militant groups to enable anti-Coalition attacks. Tehran has been responsible for at least some of the increasing lethality of anti-Coalition attacks by providing Shia militants with the capability to build IEDs with explosively formed projectiles similar to those developed by Iran and Lebanese Hizballah.

Tehran's intentions to inflict pain on the United States in Iraq has been constrained by its caution to avoid giving Washington an excuse to attack it, the clerical leadership's general satisfaction with trends in Iraq, and Iran's desire to avoid chaos on its borders.

Iranian conventional military power constitutes the greatest potential threat to Persian Gulf states and a challenge to US interests. Iran is enhancing its ability to project its military power in order to threaten to disrupt the operations and reinforcement of US forces based in the region—potentially intimidating regional allies into withholding support for US policy toward Iran—and raising the costs of our regional presence for us and our allies.

Tehran also continues to support a number of terrorist groups, viewing this capability as a critical regime safeguard by deterring US and Israeli attacks, distracting and weakening Israel, and enhancing Iran's regional influence through intimidation. Lebanese Hizballah is Iran's main terrorist ally, which—although focused on its agenda in Lebanon and supporting anti-Israeli Palestinian terrorists—has a worldwide support network and is capable of attacks against US interests if it feels its Iranian patron is threatened. Tehran also supports Palestinian Islamic Jihad and other groups in the Persian Gulf, Central and South Asia, and elsewhere.

## NORTH KOREA

North Korea claims to have nuclear weapons—a claim that we assess is probably true—and has threatened to proliferate these weapons abroad. Thus, like Iran, North Korea threatens international security and is located in a historically volatile region. Its aggressive deployment posture threatens our allies in South Korea and US troops on the peninsula. Pyongyang sells conventional weapons to Africa, Asia, and the Middle East, and has sold ballistic missiles to several Middle Eastern countries, further destabilizing regions already embroiled in conflict. And it produces and smuggles abroad counterfeit US currency, as well as narcotics, and other contraband.

Pyongyang sees nuclear weapons as the best way to deter superior US and South Korean forces, to ensure regime security, as a lever for economic gain, and as a source of prestige. Accordingly, the North remains a major challenge to the global nuclear nonproliferation regimes. We do not know the conditions under which the North would be willing to fully relinquish its nuclear weapons and its weapons program. Nor do we see signs of organized opposition to the regime among North Korea's political or military elite.

## GOVERNANCE, POLITICAL INSTABILITY, AND DEMOCRATIZATION

Good governance and, over the long term, progress toward democratization are crucial factors in navigating through the period of international turmoil and transition that commenced with the end of the Cold War and that will continue well into the future. In the absence of effective governance and reform, political instability often compromises our security interests while threatening new democracies and pushing flailing states into failure.

I will now review those states of greatest concern to the United States, framing my discussion within the context of trends and developments in their respective regions.

### MIDDLE EAST and SOUTH ASIA

**Middle East.** The tensions between autocratic regimes, extremism, and democratic forces extend well beyond our earlier discussion about Iran, Iraq and Afghanistan to other countries in the Middle East. Emerging political competition and the energizing of public debate on the role of democracy and Islam in the region could lead to the opening of political systems and development of civic institutions, providing a possible bulwark against extremism. But the path to change is far from assured. Forces for change are vulnerable to fragmentation and longstanding regimes are increasingly adept at using both repression and limited reforms to moderate political pressures to assure their survival.

We continue to watch closely events in **Syria**, a pivotal— but generally unhelpful—player in a troubled region. Despite the

Syrian military withdrawal from Lebanon last year, Damascus still meddles in its internal affairs, seeks to undercut prospects for an Arab-Israeli peace, and has failed to crackdown consistently on militant infiltration into Iraq. By aligning itself with Iran, the Bashar al-Asad regime is signaling its rejection of the Western world. Over the coming year, the Syrian regime could face internal challenges as various pressures—especially the fallout of the UN investigation into the assassination of the former Lebanese Prime Minister— raise questions about President Bashar al-Asad's judgment and leadership capacity.

Syria's exit from **Lebanon** has created political opportunities in Beirut, but sectarian tensions—especially the sense among Shia that they are underrepresented in the government—and Damascus's meddling persist. Bombings since March targeting anti-Syria politicians and journalists have fueled sectarian animosities.

**Egypt** held presidential and legislative elections for the first time with multiple presidential candidates in response to internal and external pressures for democratization. The Egyptian public, however, remains discontented by economic conditions, the Arab-Israeli problem, the US presence in Iraq, and insufficient political freedoms.

**Saudi Arabia's** crackdown on al-Qa'ida has prevented major terrorist attacks in the Kingdom for more than a year and degraded the remnants of the terror network's Saudi-based leadership, manpower, access to weapons, and operational capability. These developments, the Kingdom's smooth leadership transition and high oil prices have eased, but not eliminated, concerns about stability.

**HAMAS**'s performance in last week's election ushered in a period of great uncertainty as President Abbas, the Israelis, and the rest of the world determine how to deal with a majority party in the Palestinian Legislative Council that conducts and supports terrorism and refuses to recognize or negotiate with Israel. The election, however, does not necessarily mean that the search for peace between Israel and the Palestinians is halted irrevocably. The vote garnered by HAMAS may have been cast more *against* the

Fatah government than *for* the HAMAS program of rejecting Israel. In any case, HAMAS now must contend with Palestinian public opinion that has over the years has supported the two-state solution.

## SOUTH ASIA

Many of our most important interests intersect in **Pakistan**. The nation is a frontline partner in the war on terror, having captured several al-Qa'ida leaders, but also remains a major source of extremism that poses a threat to Musharraf, to the US, and to neighboring India and Afghanistan. Musharraf faces few political challenges in his dual role as President and Chief of Army Staff, but has made only limited progress moving his country toward democracy. Pakistan retains a nuclear force outside the Treaty on the Non-Proliferation of Nuclear Weapons and not subject to full-scope IAEA safeguards and has been both recipient and source— via A.Q. Khan's proliferation activities—of nuclear weapons-related technologies. Pakistan's national elections scheduled for 2007 will be a key benchmark to determine whether the country is continuing to make progress in its democratic transition.

Since **India and Pakistan** approached the brink of war in 2002, their peace process has lessened tensions and both appear committed to improving the bilateral relationship. A number of confidence-building measures, including new transportation links, have helped sustain the momentum.    Still, the fact that both have nuclear weapons and missiles to deliver them entails obvious and dangerous risks of escalation.

## EURASIA

In **Russia**, President Putin's drive to centralize power and assert control over civil society, growing state control over strategic sectors of the economy, and the persistence of widespread corruption raise questions about the country's direction. Russia could become a more inward-looking and difficult interlocutor for the United States over the next several years. High profits from exports of oil and gas and perceived policy successes at home and abroad have bolstered Moscow's confidence.

Russia probably will work with the United States on shared interests such as counterterrorism, counternarcotics, and counterproliferation. However, growing suspicions about Western intentions and Moscow's desire to demonstrate its independence and defend its own interests may make it harder to cooperate with Russia on areas of concern to the United States.

Now, let me briefly examine the rest of post-Soviet Eurasia where the results in the past year have been mixed.

Many of the former Soviet republics are led by autocratic, corrupt, clan-based regimes whose political stability is based on different levels of repression; yet, at the same time, we have seen in Georgia, Ukraine, and Kyrgyzstan the emergence of grassroots forces for change.

**Central Asia** remains plagued by political stagnation and repression, rampant corruption, widespread poverty and widening socio-economic inequalities, and other problems that nurture nascent radical sentiment and terrorism. In the worst, but not implausible case, central authority in one or more of these states could evaporate as rival clans or regions vie for power—opening the door to an expansion of terrorist and criminal activity on the model of failed states like Somalia and, when it was under Taliban rule, Afghanistan.

## LATIN AMERICA

A gradual consolidation and improvement of democratic institutions is the dominant trend in much of Latin America. By the year's end, ten countries will have held presidential elections and none is more important to US interests than the contest in Mexico in July. Mexico has taken advantage of NAFTA and its economy has become increasingly integrated with the US and Canada. Committed democrats in countries like Brazil and Chile are promoting economic growth and poverty alleviation. And despite battling persistent insurgent and paramilitary forces with considerable success, Colombia remains committed to keeping on a democratic path. Nonetheless, radical populist figures in some countries advocate statist economic policies and show little respect for democratic institutions.

In **Venezuela**, President Chavez, if he wins reelection later this year, appears ready to use his control of the legislature and other institutions to continue to stifle the opposition, reduce press freedom, and entrench himself through measures that are technically legal, but which nonetheless constrict democracy. We expect Chavez to deepen his relationship with Castro (Venezuela provides roughly two-thirds of that island's oil needs on preferential credit terms). He also is seeking closer economic, military, and diplomatic ties with Iran and North Korea. Chavez has scaled back counternarcotics cooperation with the US.

Increased oil revenues have allowed Chavez to embark on an activist foreign policy in Latin America that includes providing oil at favorable repayment rates to gain allies, using newly created media outlets to generate support for his Bolivarian goals, and meddling in the internal affairs of his neighbors by backing particular candidates for elective office.

In **Bolivia**, South America's poorest country with the hemisphere's highest proportion of indigenous people, the victory of Evo Morales reflects the public's lack of faith in traditional political parties and institutions. Since his election he appears to have moderated his earlier promises to nationalize the hydrocarbons industry and cease coca eradication. But his administration continues to send mixed signals regarding its intentions.

**Haiti's** interim government is the weakest in the hemisphere and the security climate could continue to deteriorate due to slum gang violence. A failure to renew the UN mandate would greatly increase the risk of a complete nationwide breakdown of public order, intensifying migration pressures. The perception among would-be migrants that the US migration policy is tough is the most important factor in deterring Haitians from fleeing their country.

## SOUTHEAST ASIA

Southeast Asia includes vibrant, diverse, and emerging democracies looking to the United States as a source of stability, wealth, and leadership. But it is also home to terrorism, separatist aspirations, crushing poverty, ethnic violence, and religious divisions. Burma remains a dictatorship, and Cambodia is retreating from progress on democracy and human rights made in the 1990s. The region is particularly at risk from avian flu, which I will discuss at greater length in a moment. Al-Qa'ida-affiliated and other extremist groups are present in many countries, although effective government policies have limited their growth and impact.

The prospects for democratic consolidation are relatively bright in **Indonesia**, the country with the world's largest Muslim population. President Yudhoyono is moving forward to crack down on corruption, professionalize the military, bring peace to the long-troubled province of Aceh, and implement economic reforms. On the counterterrorism side, Indonesian authorities have detained or killed significant elements of Jemaah Islamiya (JI), the al Qa'ida-linked terrorist group, but JI remains a tough foe.

The **Philippines** remains committed to democracy despite political turbulence over alleged cheating in the 2004 election and repeated rumors of coup plots. Meanwhile, Manila continues to struggle with the thirty-five year old Islamic and Communist rebellions, and faces growing concerns over the presence of JI terrorists in the south.

Thailand is searching for a formula to contain violence instigated by ethnic -Malay Muslim separatist groups in the far southern provinces. In 2005, the separatists showed signs of stronger organization and more lethal and brutal tactics targeting the government and Buddhist population in the south.

## AFRICA

Some good news is coming out of Africa. The continent is

enjoying real economic growth after a decade of declining per capita income. The past decade has also witnessed a definite, albeit gradual, trend toward greater democracy, openness, and multiparty elections. In **Liberia,** the inauguration of Ellen Johnson Sirleaf as President, following a hotly contested multi-party election, was a positive harbinger of a return to democratic rule in a battered nation.

Yet, in much of the continent, humanitarian crises, instability, and conflict persist. Overlaying these enduring threats are the potential spread of jihadist ideology among disaffected Muslim populations and the region's growing importance as a source of energy. We are most concerned about Sudan and Nigeria.

The signing of a Comprehensive Peace Agreement in **Sudan** last year was a major achievement, but the new Government of National Unity is being tested by the continuing conflict in Darfur, and instability in Chad is spilling over into western Sudan, further endangering humanitarian aid workers and assistance supply lines. Gains in stabilizing and improving the conditions in Darfur could be reversed if the new instability goes unchecked.

The most important election on the African horizon will be held in spring 2007 in **Nigeria,** the continent's most populous country and largest oil producer. The vote has the potential to reinforce a democratic trend away from military rule—or it could lead to major disruption in a nation suffering frequent ethno-religious violence, criminal activity, and rampant corruption. Speculation that President Obasanjo will try to change the constitution so he can seek a third term in office is raising political tensions and, if proven true, threatens to unleash major turmoil and conflict. Such chaos in Nigeria could lead to disruption of oil supply, secessionist moves by regional governments, major refugee flows, and instability elsewhere in West Africa.

## GLOBALIZATION AND RISING ACTORS

To one degree or another, all nations are affected by the phenomenon known as globalization. Many see the United States as globalization's primary beneficiary, but the developments subsumed under its rubric operate largely beyond the control of all countries. Small, medium, and large states are both gaining and losing through technological and economic developments at a rate of speed unheard of in human history.

Such recalibrations in regional and global standing usually emerge in the wake of war. But globalization isn't a war, even though its underside— fierce competition for global energy reserves, discrepancies between rich and poor, criminal networks that create and feed black markets in drugs and even human beings, and the rapid transmission of disease—has the look of a silent but titanic global struggle.

One major recalibration of the global order enabled by globalization is the shift of world economic momentum and energy to greater Asia—led principally by explosive economic growth in China and the growing concentration of world manufacturing activity in and around it. India, too, is emerging as a new pole of greater Asia's surging economic and political power. These two Asian giants comprise fully a third of the world's population—a huge labor force eager for modern work, supported by significant scientific and technological capabilities, and an army of new claimants on the world's natural resources and capital.

## CHINA

China is a rapidly rising power with steadily expanding global reach that may become a peer competitor to the United States at some point. Consistent high rates of economic growth, driven by exploding foreign trade, have increased Beijing's political influence abroad and fueled a military modernization program that has steadily increased Beijing's force projection capabilities.

Chinese foreign policy is currently focused on the country's immediate periphery, including Southeast and Central Asia, where Beijing hopes to make economic inroads, increase political influence, and prevent a backlash against its rise. Its rhetoric toward

Taiwan has been less inflammatory since Beijing passed its "anti-secession" law last spring. China has been reaching out to the opposition parties on Taiwan and making economic overtures designed to win favor with the Taiwan public—although Beijing still refuses to deal with the elected leader in Taipei.

Beijing also has expanded diplomatic and economic interaction with other major powers—especially Russia and the EU—and begun to increase its presence in Africa and Latin America.

China's military is vigorously pursuing a modernization program: a full suite of modern weapons and hardware for a large proportion of its overall force structure; designs for a more effective operational doctrine at the tactical and theater level; training reforms; and wide-ranging improvements in logistics, administration, financial management, mobilization, and other critical support functions.

Beijing's biggest challenge is to sustain growth sufficient to keep unemployment and rural discontent from rising to destabilizing levels and to maintain increases in living standards. To do this, China must solve a number of difficult economic and legal problems, improve the education system, reduce environmental degradation, and improve governance by combating corruption.

Indeed, China's rise may be hobbled by systemic problems and the Communist Party's resistance to the demands for political participation that economic growth generates. Beijing's determination to repress real or perceived challenges—from dispossessed peasants to religious organizations—could lead to serious instability at home and less effective policies abroad.

## INDIA

Rapid economic growth and increasing technological competence are securing India's leading role in South Asia, while helping India to realize its longstanding ambition to become a global power. India's growing confidence on the world stage as a result of its increasingly globalized business activity will make New Delhi a more effective partner for the United States, but also a more formidable player on issues such as those before the WTO.

New Delhi seeks to play a key role in fostering democracy in the region, especially in Nepal and Bangladesh, and will continue to be a reliable ally against global terrorism, in part because India has been a frequent target for Islamic terrorists, mainly in Kashmir. India seeks better relations with its two main rivals —Pakistan and China—recognizing that its regional disputes with them are hampering its larger goals on the world stage. Nevertheless, like China, India is using its newfound wealth and technical capabilities to extend its military reach.

On the economic front, as Indian multinationals become more prevalent, they will offer competition and cooperation with the United States in fields such as energy, steel, and pharmaceuticals. New Delhi's pursuit of energy to fuel its rapidly growing economy adds to pressure on world prices and increases the likelihood that it will seek to augment its programs in nuclear power, coal technologies, and petroleum exploration. Like Pakistan, India is outside the Nonproliferation Treaty.

## THREATS TO GLOBAL ENERGY SECURITY

World energy markets seem certain to remain tight for the foreseeable future. Robust global economic expansion is pushing strong energy demand growth and—combined with instability in several oil producing regions—is increasing the geopolitical leverage of key energy producer states such as Iran, Saudi Arabia, Russia, and Venezuela. At the same time, the pursuit of secure energy supplies has become a much more significant driver of foreign policy in countries where energy demand growth is surging—particularly China and India.

The changing global oil and gas market has encouraged Russia's assertiveness with Ukraine and Georgia, Iran's nuclear brinksmanship, and the populist "petro-diplomacy" of Venezuela's

Hugo Chavez. Russia's recent but short-lived curtailment of natural gas deliveries to Ukraine temporarily reduced gas supplies to much of Europe and is an example of how energy can be used as both a political and economic tool. The gas disruption alarmed Europeans—reminding them of their dependence on Russian gas—and refocused debate on alternative energy sources.

Foreign policy frictions, driven by energy security concerns, are likely to be fed by continued global efforts of Chinese and Indian firms to ink new oilfield development deals and to purchase stakes in foreign oil and gas properties. Although some of these moves may incrementally increase oil sector investment and global supplies, others may bolster countries such as Iran, Syria, and Sudan that pose significant US national security risks or foreign policy challenges. For example, in Venezuela, Chavez is attempting to diversify oil exports away from the US.

## THE SECURITY THREAT FROM NARCOTICS TRAFFICKING

In addition to the central US national security interest in stemming the flow of drugs to this country, there are two international threats related to narcotics: first, the potential threat from an intersection of narcotics and extremism; and second, the threat from the impact of drugs on those ineffective and unreliable nation states about which we are so concerned.

Although the worldwide trafficking-terrorist relationship is limited, the scope of these ties has grown modestly in recent years. A small number of terrorist groups engage the services of or accept donations from criminals, including narcotics traffickers, to help raise operational funds. While the revenue realized by extremists appears small when compared to that of the dedicated trafficking organizations, even small amounts of income can finance destructive acts of terror.

The tie between drug trafficking and extremism is strongest in Colombia and Afghanistan. Both of Colombia's insurgencies and most of its paramilitary groups reap substantial benefits from cocaine transactions. In Afghanistan, the Taliban and Hizb-i Islami Gulbudin gain at least some of their financial support from their ties to local opiates traffickers. Ties between trafficking and extremists elsewhere are less robust and profitable. North African extremists involved in the 2004 Madrid train bombings reportedly used drug income to buy their explosives.

Most major international organized crime groups have kept terrorists at arm's length, although some regional criminal gangs have supplied fraudulent or altered travel documents, moved illicit earnings, or provided other criminal services to members of insurgent or terrorist groups for a fee.

Narcotics traffickers—and other organized criminals— typically do not want to see governments toppled but thrive in states where governments are weak, vulnerable to or seeking out corruption, and unable—or unwilling—to consistently enforce the rule of law. Nonetheless, a vicious cycle can develop in which a weakened government enables criminals to dangerously undercut the state's credibility and authority with the consequence that the investment climate suffers, economic growth withers, black market activity rises, and fewer resources are available for civil infrastructure and governance.

We are particularly concerned about this cycle in countries on the other side of the world, such as Afghanistan, Kyrgyzstan, and Burma, and those close to home, such as in Haiti, Jamaica, and Mexico. About 90 percent of detected cocaine destined for the US was smuggled through the Mexico– Central America corridor; nearly all Mexican heroin is for the US market; and Mexico is the primary foreign supplier of marijuana and methamphetamine to the US.

## THE THREAT FROM PANDEMICS AND EPIDEMICS

In the 21$^{st}$ century, our Intelligence Community has expanded the definition of bio -threats to the US beyond weapons to naturally occurring pandemics. The most pressing infectious disease challenge facing the US is the potential emergence of a new and deadly avian influenza strain, which could cause a worldwide outbreak, or pandemic. International health experts worry that avian influenza could become transmissible among humans, threatening the health and lives of millions of people around the globe. There are many unknowns about avian flu, but even the specter of an outbreak could have significant effects on the international economy, whole societies, military operations, critical infrastructure, and diplomatic relations.

Avian flu is not something we can fight alone. An effective response to it is highly dependent on the openness of affected nations in reporting outbreaks where and when they occur. But for internal political reasons, a lack of response capability, or disinclination to regard avian influenza as a significant threat, some countries are not forthcoming. In close coordination with the Department of Health and Human Services, the Intelligence Community therefore is tracking a number of key countries that are—or could be—especially prone to avian influenza outbreaks and where we cannot be confident that adequate information will be available through open sources. The IC also coordinates closely with the Department of Homeland Security (DHS) and provides input to the national Bio Surveillance Integration System at DHS.

**Conclusion**

Each of the major intelligence challenges I have discussed today is affected by the accelerating change and transnational interplay that are the hallmarks of 21st century globalization. As a direct result, collecting, analyzing, and acting on solid intelligence have become increasingly difficult. To meet these new and reconfigured challenges, we need to work hand-in -hand with other responsible nations. Fortunately, the vast majority of governments in the world are responsible and responsive, but those that are not are neither few in numbers nor lacking in material resources and geopolitical influence.

The powerful critiques of this Committee, the 9/11 Commission, and the WMD Commission, framed by statute in the Intelligence Reform and Terrorism Prevention Act of 2004 and taken to heart by the dedicated professionals of our Intelligence Community, have helped make us better prepared and more vigilant than we were on that terrible day in September 2001. But from an intelligence perspective, we cannot rest. We must transform our intelligence capabilities and cultures by fully integrating them from local law enforcement through national authorities in Washington to combatant commanders overseas. The more thoroughly we do that, the more clearly we will be able to see the threats lurking in the shadow of the future and ward them off.

Thank you very much.

# APPENDIX E

# SIX SCRIPTURAL STEPS TO SALVATION

Men still cry, "What must I do to be saved?" The Bible provides a clear answer. Here are the six Scriptural steps which all must take to pass from death unto life:

1. ACKNOWLEDGE: "For all have sinned and come short of the glory of God" (Romans 3:23). "God be merciful to me a sinner" (Luke 18:13). You must acknowledge in the light of God's Word that you are a sinner.

2. REPENT: "Except ye repent, ye shall all likewise perish" (Luke 13:3). "Repent ye therefore, and be converted, that your sins may be blotted out" (Acts 3:19). You must see the awfulness of sin and then repent of it. What does it mean to repent? According to the dictionary, to repent is "to turn from sin and dedicate oneself to the amendment of one's life."[179] (*Amend* means to put right, to change or modify for the better.)

3. CONFESS: "If we confess our sins, he is faithful and just to forgive us our sins, and to cleanse us from all unrighteousness" (1 John 1:9). "With the mouth confession is made unto salvation"

(Romans 10:10). Confess not to men but to God.

4. FORSAKE: "Let the wicked forsake his way, and the unrighteous man has thoughts: and let him return unto the Lord . . . for he will abundantly pardon" (Isaiah 55:7). Sorrow for sin is not enough in itself. We must want to be done with it once and for all. "By faith Moses, when he was come to years, refused to be called the son of Pharaoh's daughter; Choosing rather to suffer affliction with the people of God, than to enjoy the pleasures of sin for a season" (Hebrews 11:24-25). By faith, choose to forsake the pleasures of sin. They are not worth spending eternity in hell.

5. BELIEVE: "For God so loved the world, that he gave his only begotten Son, that whosoever believeth in him should not perish, but have everlasting life" (John 3:16). "If thou shalt confess with thy mouth the Lord Jesus, and shalt believe in thine heart that God hath raised Him from the dead, thou shalt be saved" (Romans 10:9). Believe in the finished work of Christ on the Cross.

6. RECEIVE: "He came unto his own, and his own received him not. But as many as received him, to them gave he power to become the sons of God, even to them that believe on his name" (John 1: 11, 12). Christ must be received personally into the heart by faith, if the experience of the New Birth is to be yours.

The Bible says "That if thou shalt confess with thy mouth the Lord Jesus, and shalt believe in thine heart that God hath raised him from the dead, thou shalt be saved. For with the heart man believeth unto righteousness; and with the mouth confession is made unto salvation. For the scripture saith, Whosoever believeth on him shall not be ashamed" (Romans 10:9-11).

Why not pray this prayer right now?

*Heavenly Father, I know that I am guilty of sin and*
*my sins have separated me from You.*
*I ask You to forgive me for all of my sins and help*
*me to live a life that pleases You.*
*I believe that Jesus Christ died for my sins, shed His*

*blood to cleanse me from sin, was resurrected from
the dead, and hears this prayer.
I now invite You, Jesus, to become the Lord of my
life, to reign in my heart from this day forward.
I receive You as my personal Lord and Savior, and
confess with my mouth that **Jesus is my Lord**.
Amen.*

When you prayed this prayer, please let me know about it so that we may rejoice together. Write to me at Chris Panos, P. 0. Box 3333, Houston, Texas U.S.A. 77253-3333. Or email me at chrispanos@chrispanos.com. And of course you're invited to visit my web site at www.chrispanos.com.

*NOTES*

# *Notes*

[1] Jay Solomon, "Negroponte Calls al Qaeda, Iran, North Korea Top Concerns." *The Wall Street Journal Online*, February 3, 2006.

[2] US State Department, "State Sponsors of Terror Overview," http://www.state.gov/documents/organization/65476.pdf

[3] The Islamic Republic of Ir Broadcasting (IRIB) and Iran's official FAR news agency, as cited by Yaakov Lappin in "Iran: Israel, US will soon die," ynet news.com, January 23, 2007. http://www.ynetnews.com/articles/0,7340,L-3356154,00.html.

[4] Associated Press, "New Intelligence Report Finds Al Qaeda Focused on U.S. Strike," *The Wall Street Journal Online*, July 12, 2007 6:20 p.m. http://online.wsj.com/article/SB118425569222864774

[5] Reuters, "Satellite Images Suggest New Tunnels Near Iranian Nuclear Plant," *The New York Times*, July 10, 2007.

[6] Alan Cowell and Raymond Bonner, "In Intense Hunt for Bombers, Britain Sees Qaeda Link," *The New York Times*, July 2, 2007.

[7] Yaakov Katz, "Security and Defense: Explosive challenges – on all fronts," The Jerusalem Post, July 13, 2007, updated July 14. http://www.jpost.com/servlet/Satellite?cid=1184168553291&pagename=JPost%2FJPArticle%2FShowFull

[8] Nazih Siddiq, Reuters Foundation AlertNet, "Army pounds Lebanon camp, soldier deaths near 100." July 14, 2007. http://www.alertnet.org/thenews/newsdesk/L14521002.htm

[9] Reuters Foundation *AlertNet*, "About 200,000 troops in SE Turkey-security sources," July 13, 2007. http://www.alertnet.org/thenews/newsdesk/L13537048.htm

[10] Reuters, "Russia warns it may quit key arms pact in 5 months," July 14, 2007. http://www.reuters.com/article/topNews/idUSL1439340220070714?pageNumber=2

[11] "Russia warns it may quit key arms pact in 5 months"

[12] Joint Statement by President Bush, President Fox, and Prime Minister Martin, "Security and Prosperity Partnership of North America," www.whitehouse.gov, March 23, 2005. http://www.whitehouse.gov/news/releases/2005/03/20050323-2.html

[13] "Congressman: Superhighway about North American Union," *WorldNetDaily*, October 30, 2006. http://www.worldnetdaily.com/news/article.asp?ARTICLE_ID=52684.

[14] "Mexico Ambassador: We need N. American Union in 8 years," *WorldNetDaily*, November 5, 2006. http://www.worldnetdaily.com/news/article.asp?ARTICLE_ID=52788.

[15] "Bush doesn't think America should be an actual place," *WorldNetDaily*, November 19, 2006.
http://www.worldnetdaily.com/news/article.asp?ARTICLE_ID=53023

[16] Jerry Mazza, "An American Union under Bush," *Online Journal*, May 23, 2007. http://www.onlinejournal.com/artman/publish/article_1883.shtml

[17] Ian R.K: Paisley, M.P., M.E.P., "The Vacant Seat Number 666 in the European Parliament," *Free Republic*, August 31, 2001.
http://www.freerepublic.com/focus/news/742553/posts

[18] *count down u.s.a*, "The Tower of Babel" downloaded July 22, 2007.
http://nextcrusade.com/eu.html

[19] "The Vacant Seat Number 666 in the European Parliament"

[20] "Profile: Mahmoud Ahmadinejad" *Aljazeera.net*, June 19, 2005.
http://english.aljazeera.net/NR/exeres/91109A0C-83F4-438F-9CC1-52DF6936CC6B.htm.

[21] "Ahmadinejad is a 'miracle', says new book" *Daily Times*, May 22, 2006.
http://www.dailytimes.com.pk/default.asp?page=2006%5C05%5C22%5Cstory_22-5-2006_pg4_16.

[22] *Merriam-Webster Online Dictionary*.
http://www.merriamwebster.com/dictionary/antichrist.

[23] Scott Peterson, "Waiting for the rapture in Iran," *The Christian Science Monitor*, December 21, 2005. http://www.csmonitor.com/2005/1221/p01s04-wome.html.

[24] "Ahmadinejad: Wipe Israel off map" *Al Jazeera.net*, October 26, 2005.
http://english.aljazeera.net/NR/exeres/15E6BF77-6F91-46EE-A4B5-A3CE0E9957EA.htm.

[25] Steve Schippert, "Understanding Ahmadinejad," *ThreatsWatch,* November 28, 2005. http://analysis.threatswatch.org/ 2005/11/understanding-ahmadinejad.

[26] Michael Slackman, "Iran Chief Eclipses Clerics as He Consolidates Power," *The New York Times*, May 28, 2006.

[27] "Waiting for the rapture in Iran"

[28] "Profile: Mahmoud Ahmadinejad"

[29] "Iran victor 'kidnap role' probe," *BBC News*, June 30, 2005 at
http://news.bbc.co.uk/2/hi/middle_east/4636955.stm.

[30] "Understanding Ahmadinejad"

[31] Lindsey Hilsum, "preparing Iran for judgement day," NewStatesman, Monday December 5, 2005. http://www.newstatesman.com/200512050014.

[32] Anton La Guardia, "'Divine mission' driving Iran's new leader," *Telegraph*, January 14, 2006. http://www.telegraph.co.uk/news/main.jhtml?xml=/news/2006/01/14/wiran14.xml&sSheet=/news/2006/01/14/ixworld.html.

[33] David Bukay, editor, *Muhammad's Monsters: A Comprehensive Guide to Radical Islam for Western Audiences*, "Islamic Fundamentalism and the Arab Political Culture" (Green Forest, AR: Balfour Books, 2004), p. 14.

[34] Robert Tracinski, "We Are All Israelis Now," September 18, 2001. http://www.aynrand.org/site/News2?JServSessionIdr006=hn08b4f994.app14b&page=NewsArticle&id=5179&news_iv_ctrl=1021.

[35] Charles Selengut, "Sacred Visions and Religious Terror: The Case of Islam" in *Muhammad's Monsters*, p. 42.

[36] Walid Phares, *Future Jihad* (New York: Palgrave MacMillan, 2005), p. 134.

[37] *Future Jihad*, pp. 134-135.

[38] Abdullah Al Araby, *Islam Review*, "Lying in Islam," http://www.islamreview.com/articles/lying.shtml.

[39] William P. Welty, "The Lie is Different at Every Level" June 14, 2004. http://www.israelnationalnews.com/print.php3?what=article&id=3798.

[40] Dr. Ahmed Yousuf Abu Halabiya, PA TV, July 28, 2000, quoted by *Palestinian Media Watch: A Self Portrait of Palestinian Society*, "Denying Israel's Right to Exist and Anticipating its Destruction," written and compiled by Itamar Marcus. http://www.pmw.org.il/Denying%20Israel's%20right%20to%20exist.htm.

[41] There are many variations of this saying, including: "I against my brothers, I and my brothers against my cousins, I, my brothers and cousins against the stranger"; "My brother and I against my cousin, my cousin and I against the stranger"; "My brother and I against my cousin, and my cousin and I against the stranger" plus a number of others.

[42] Jamie Glazov, "Symposium: Darfur – Islam's Killing Fields," *Front Page Magazine*, September 10, 2004. http://www.frontpagemag.com/Articles/ReadArticle.asp?ID=15026.

[43] Jon Lewis, as quoted in "Symposium: Darfur – Islam's Killing Fields"

[44] *Future Jihad*, p. 91

[45] A.S. Abraham and George Haddad, *The Warriors of God* (Bristol, IN: Wyndham Hall Press, 1989), p. 1, as quoted in *Muhammad's Monsters*, p.49.

[46] Shaul Shay and Yoram Schweitzer "The 'Afghan Alumni' Terrorism: Islamic Militants against the Rest of the World", November 6, 2000. http://www.ict.org.il/articles/articledet.cfm?articleid=140.

[47] Ryan Jones, "Hamas: Islam will rule the world," *Jerusalem Newswire*, February 8, 2006. http://www.jnewswire.com/library/article.php?articleid=985.

[48] "The Lie is Different at Every Level"

[49] *The 9/11 Commission Report*, p. 64 (http://i.a.cnn.net/cnn/US/resources/9.11.report/911Report.pdf); available for download at http://edition.cnn.com/2004/US/07/22/9.11.full.report/.

[50] Hani Shukrallah, "We are all Iraqis now"; *The Guardian*, March 27, 2003. http://www.guardian.co.uk/Iraq/Story/0,2763,922751,00.html.

[51] Wissam S. Yafi, "Arab intelligentsia walks a tightrope," *The Daily Star*, 5/14/03, posted on Al-Jazeerah.info. http://www.aljazeerah.info/

Opinion%20editorials/2003%20Opinion%20Editorials/May/14-b%20o/Arab%20
intelligentsia%20walks%20a%20tightrope,%20Wissam%20S%20Yafi.htm.

[52] "Virgins? What virgins?" The Guardian, January 12, 2002.
http://www.guardian.co.uk/saturday_review/story/0,3605,631332,00.html.

[53] Roger Cohen, "From Wounded Pride, a Deadly Rage Explodes," *International Herald Tribune*, January 11, 2006.

[54] George Friedman, *America's Secret War* (New York: Broadway Books, 2004), p. 14-15.

[55] *America's Secret War*, p. 26

[56] *America's Secret War*, p. 29

[57] *America's Secret War*, p. 21

[58] *Future Jihad*, pp. 122-123.

[59] Kenneth R. Timmerman, "U.S. dropped ball in terror war in '83," *World Net Daily*, December 23, 2003. http://hellodiplomatic.com/nx.asp?noti=28734

[60] Rohan Gunaratna, "The Rise and Decline of Al Qaeda," July 9, 2003, Statement of Rohan Gunaratna to the National Commission on Terrorist Attacks Upon the United States. http://www.9-11commission.gov/hearings/hearing3/witness_gunaratna.htm

[61] B. Raman, "Pakistan & Dangers of Nuclear Jihad," South Asia Analysis Group website, January 27, 2004. http://www.saag.org/papers10/paper904.html

[62] Ibid.

[63] Ibid.

[64] Ibid.

[65] Nicholas D. Kristoff, "An American Hiroshima," *The New York Times*, August 11, 2004.

[66] "Al-Qaida's U.S. nuke targets" *G2 Bulletin*, July 12, 2005, available to subscribers at
http://www.g2bulletin.com/index.php?fa=PAGE.view&pageId=809

[67] "MI6 confirms bin Laden's nukes," G2 Bulletin, April 29, 2006, available to subscribers at
http://www.g2bulletin.com/index.php?fa=PAGE.view&pageId=1044.

[68] "Al-Qaida's nuclear efforts: 'sophisticated, professional'" *World Net Daily*, August 22, 2005.
http://www.worldnetdaily.com/news/article.asp?ARTICLE_ID=45888.

[69] Ryan Mauro, "Al-Qaeda's Hidden Arsenal and Sponsors: Interview with Hamid Mi," *WorldThreats.com*.
http://www.worldthreats.com/general_information/aqarsenal.htm

[70] Department of Homeland Security, "Emergencies & Disasters."
http://www.dhs.gov/dhspublic/display?theme=14&content=446

[71] U.S. Senator Jon Kyl, "One Way We Could Lose the War on Terror," March 14, 2005. Press release available at
http://www.senate.gov/member/az/kyl/general/record_print.cfm?id=233434.

[72] Jack Spencer, "The Electromagnetic Pulse Commission Warns of an Old Threat with a New Face," The Heritage Foundation, August 3, 2004. http://www.heritage.org/Research/NationalSecurity/bg1784.cfm

[73] *Ain-Al-Yaqeen*, March 19, 2004. http://www.ain-al-yaqeen.com/issues/20040319/feat2en.htm

[74] Ryan Jones, "Hamas: Islam will rule the world," *Jerusalem Newswire*, February 8, 2006. http://www.jnewswire.com/library/article.php?articleid=985

[75] Reuven and Mary Doron, "Gaza – The Fuse Is Lit" June 16, 2007, *One New Man Call*[OneNewManMail@aol.com]

[76] "Gaza – The Fuse Is Lit"

[77] Mamoun Fandy, "Avoiding the Next Generation of Al-Qaeda?" *Third public hearing of the National Commission on Terrorist Attacks Upon the United States.* http://www.9-11commission.gov/hearings/hearing3/witness_fandy.htm

[78] Walid Phares, "CV of Dr. Walid A. Phares" Nov. 8, 2005 http://www.walidphares.com

[79] *Future Jihad*, p. 19

[80] Rosemary McDonough, "The Yale Jihad" *The Evening Bulletin*, June 19, 2006. http://www.zwire.com/site/news.cfm?newsid=16249062&BRD=2737&PAG=461&dept_id=576940&rfi=6

[81] "King Fahd as monarch (Screen 4 of 5)" viewed 4/30/06 at http://www.kingfahdbinabdulaziz.com/main/b33.htm

[82] Center for Religious Freedom, "New Report on Saudi Government Publications" January 28, 2005. http://www.freedomhouse.org/religion/news/bn2005/bn-2005-01-28.htm

[83] Center for Religious Freedom, *Saudi Publications on Hate Ideology Invade American Mosques* (Washington, DC: 2005 Center for Religious Freedom) available for download at http://www.freedomhouse.org/religion/pdfdocs/FINAL%20FINAL.pdf.

[84] George P. Schultz, "Terrorism: What Must Be Done," *Hoover Digest* 2002 – No. 2 – Spring Issue at http://www.hooverdigest.org/022/shultz.html

[85] Jamie Glazov, "Saudi Arabia: Friend or Foe?" *FrontPageMagazine.com*, September 9, 2002. http://www.frontpagemag.com/Articles/ReadArticle.asp?ID=2852.

[86] Laurent Murawiec, *Princes of Darkness.* Lanham, Maryland: Rowman & Littlefield Publishers, Inc., 2003, p.51.

[87] "Disabled Child in suicide attack," *Evening Standard*, January 31, 2005, at http://www.thisislondon.co.uk/news/articles/16278831

[88] "Avoiding the Next Generation of Al-Qaeda?"

[89] Fawaz A. Gerges, *Journey of the Jihadist: Inside Muslim Militancy.* Orlando: Harcourt, Inc. 2006, p. 12

[90] *The 9/11 Commission Report*, pp. 49-50.

[91] *The 9/11 Commission Report*, pp. 50-51.

[92] Youssef Michel Ibrahim, "The Mideast Threat That's Hard to Define," originally published on August 11, 2002 by *The Washington Post* and reprinted on the Council on Foreign Relations website, http://www.cfr.org/publication/4702/mideast_threat_thats_hard_to_define.html
[93] Michael Young, "Is Saudi Arabia A Strategic Threat: The Global Propagation Of Intolerance" November 18, 2003 (Transcript by: Federal News Service Washington, D.C. ) United States Commission on International Religious Freedom. http://www.uscirf.gov/events/hearings/2003/november/11182003_saudiThreat.html
[94] Flynt Leverett, "The Race for Iran," *The New York Times*, June 20, 2006, at http://www.nytimes.com/2006/06/20/opinion/20leverett.html?n=Top%2fNews%2fWorld%2fCountries%20and%20Territories%2fIran
[95] "Background Note: Iran," U.S. Department of State Bureau of Near Eastern Affairs, August 2005. http://www.state.gov/r/pa/ei/bgn/5314.htm
[96] Laurie Goodstein, "Iran's Bahai Religious Minority Says It Faces Raids and Arrests," *The New York Times*, June 1, 2006.
[97] Ibid
[98] BBC "Persecution in Iran." http://www.bbc.co.uk/religion/religions/bahai/history/persecution.shtml
[99] U.S. Department of Justice Federal Bureau of Investigation, "Terrorism in the United States 1999." http://www.fbi.gov/publications/terror/terror99.pdf, p. 30
[100] Dr. Rachel Ehrenfeld and Alyssa A. Lappen, *FrontPageMagazine.com*, June 16, 2006. http://www.frontpagemag.com/Articles/ReadArticle.asp?ID=22916
[101] Ibid
[102] Ibid
[103] Council on Foreign Relations, "State Sponsors: Syria." http://www.cfr.org/publication/9368/, updated December 2005.
[104] Library of Congress—Federal Research Division, "Country Profile: Afghanistan, May 2006." http://lcweb2.loc.gov/frd/cs/profiles/Afghanistan.pdf.
[105] U.S. Department of State, "Algeria: International Religious Freedom Report 2005," released by the Bureau of Democracy, Human Rights, and Labor." http://www.state.gov/g/drl/rls/irf/2005/51596.htm.
[106] U.S. Department of State, "Bahrain: International Religious Freedom Report 2005," released by the Bureau of Democracy, Human Rights, and Labor. http://www.state.gov/g/drl/rls/irf/2005/51597.htm.
[107] U.S. Department of State, "Chad: International Religious Freedom Report 2005," released by the Bureau of Democracy, Human Rights, and Labor. http://www.state.gov/g/drl/rls/irf/2005/51459.htm
[108] "Islamic revival spreads in Syria despite rule of secular Baath" *The Daily Star*, June 2, 2006. http://www.dailystar.com.lb/article.asp?edition_id=10&categ_id=2&article_id=24912

[109] Jamie Glazov, "Iraqi WMD Mystery Solved," *FrontPageMagazine*, March 2, 2006. http://www.frontpagemag.com/Articles/ReadArticle.asp?ID=21489.

[110] Georges Sada with Jim Nelson Black, *Saddam's Secrets* (Brentwood, TN: Integrity Publishers, 2006) p. 250

[111] *Saddam's Secrets,* p. 250

[112] *Saddam's Secrets*, p. 254

[113] *Saddam's Secrets*, p. 260

[114] "Dutch daily says Iraq hid weapons of mass destruction in Syria," *Financial Times*, at FinancialTimes.com, Source: De Standaard web site, Groot-Bijgaarden, in Dutch 6 Jan 04 © BBC Monitoring

[115] "Never-Before-Seen Videotaped Testimony of Former Iraqi General Confirming Iraq had WMD," WorldThreats.com, May 11, 2006, transcript available at http://www.worldthreats.com/AliWMVpage.htm

[116] John R. Bolton, Under Secretary for Arms Control and International Security, "Testimony Before the House International Relations Committee, Subcommittee on the Middle East and Central Asia, Washington, DC," September 16, 2003. http://www.state.gov/t/us/rm/24135.htm.

[117] *Saddam's Secrets*, p. 254

[118] United States Department of Defense, "Operations – Operation Iraqi Freedom" updated November 18, 2004. http://www.dod.gov/photos/Aug2003/030706-F-0000C-909.html

[119] "Iraqi aircraft 'buried in desert'" BBC.com August 1, 2003. http://news.bbc.co.uk/2/hi/middle%5Feast/3116259.stm

[120] United States Department of Defense, "Operations – Operation Iraqi Freedom" updated November 18, 2004. http://www.dod.gov/photos/Aug2003/030706-F-0000C-907.html

[121] Kathleen T. Rhem, "American Forces Pull Hidden MiG fighters out of Iraqi Desert," American Forces Press Service news release, August 6, 2003. http://www.defenselink.mil/news/Aug2003/n08062003_200308063.html

[122] Charles R. Smith, "Iraqi 'Mach 3' MiG Buried in Sand," Wednesday, August 6, 2003. www.newsmax.com/archives/articles/2003/8/6/105528.shtml

[123] Transcript: Powell: Fusion of WMD and Terrorists Must Be Prevented Fri, 20 FEB 2004 18:41:58. http://lists.state.gov/SCRIPTS/WA-USIAINFO.EXE?A2=ind0402c&L=us-iraqpolicy&H=1&O=D&P=1603

[124] Colin Powell, "Fusion of WMD and Terrorists Must Be Prevented"

[125] Daniel Pipes, "He Lied So Often, No One Believed He Removed WMD," April 25, 2005, posted on danielpipes.org as "About Those Iraqi WMD" http://www.danielpipes.org/article/3545

[126] Ibid.

[127] Charles Krauthammer, *The Weekly Standard*, May 11, 1998. Quoted in "Arab-Israeli Conflict: Basic Facts" at http://www.science.co.il/Arab-Israeli-conflict.asp

[128] Commentary by Rabbi David Kopstein, Saturday December 10, 2005, Shabbat Kislev 9, 5766 at http://www.upj.org.au/parashat_vayetze.htm
[129] "Israeli War of Independence,"
http://www.globalsecurity.org/military/world/war/israel-inde.htm
[130] Mahmoud al-Zahar, interview in *The Washington Post*, as quoted by Ryan Jones in "Hamas: Islam will rule the world," *Jerusalem Newswire*, February 8, 2006. http://www.jnewswire.com/library/article.php?articleid=985
[131] Joseph Farah, *World Net Daily*, "Myths of the Middle East," posted October 11, 2000. http://www.worldnetdaily.com/news/printer-friendly.asp?ARTICLE_ID=15066
[132] Joseph Farah, "Myths of the Middle East."
[133] Steve Meyers, "The truth about Israel, and why Christians should care," updated February 2006. http://www.radiosteve.org/exegesis/0203-israel.html
[134] Dore Gold and Jeff Helmreich, "An Answer to the new anti-Zionists: The Rights of the Jewish People to a Sovereign State in Their Historic Homeland, Jerusalem Center for Public Affairs, *Jerusalem Viewpoints*, No. 507, 21 Heshvan 5764 / 16 November 2003. http://www.jcpa.org/jl/vp507.htm.
[135] "Israel" *Wikipedia, the free encyclopedia.* http://en.wikipedia.org/wiki/Israel
[136] "Merkel: Israel's Right to Exist ''Must Never be Questioned," Deutsche Welle, May 5, 2006. http://www.dw-world.de/dw/article/0,2144,1993811,00.html
[137] "Q: Does Israel have a right to exist?"
http://www.israelipalestinianprocon.org/bin/procon/procon.cgi?database=5-B-Sub-Q1.db&command=viewone&op=t&id=13
[138] "Abba Eban on Israel's 'Right to Exist." Originally published in the New York Times, November 18, 1981, and available at
http://www.jewishvirtuallibrary.org/jsource/Quote/eban3q.html
[139] Scholars disagree on who the Hagarenes were. Were they the same as the Hagarites (1 Chronicles 5) or were they, as seems more likely, the descendents of Hagar, who was an Egyptian?
[140]
http://go.reuters.com/newsArticle.jhtml?type=worldNews&storyID=11424540&src=rss/worldNews Article dated Sat Mar 4, 2006 11:29 PM ET
[141] Abdullah Al Araby, *Islam Review*, "Lying in Islam."
[142] Emma Simpson, "Russia wields the energy weapon," BBC News, last updated Tuesday, 14 February 2006, at
http://news.bbc.co.uk/1/hi/world/europe/4708256.stm
[143] Energy statistics from "Russia wields the energy weapon"
[144] Owen Matthews and Anna Nemtova, "Partner, or Bully?" *Newsweek International*, updated 1:13 a.m. ET April 30, 2006.
http://www.msnbc.msn.com/id/12554101/site/newsweek/
[145] "Partner, or Bully?"

[146] "Russia's Energy Politics" *Washington Post* editorial, Wednesday, January 4, 2006. http://www.washingtonpost.com/wp-dyn/content/article/2006/01/03/AR2006010301283.html

[147] Paul Richter and David Holley, "Cheney Has Harsh Words for Moscow," *Los Angeles Times*, May 5, 2006

[148] "Russia, Iran call for 'energy club' of Asian States." *The Financial Express*, June 16, 2006. http://www.financialexpress.com/fe_full_story.php?content_id=130747

[149] "Russia and Turkey to Hold Joint Naval Exercises" MosNews, February 28, 2006, at http://www.mosnews.com/news/2006/02/28/jointexercise.shtml

[150] *Matthew Henry's Commentary on the Old Testament*, First Edition. Electronic Edition STEP Files Copyright © 2000, Findex.com, Inc.

[151] Don Groce, "Domestic Preparedness and Best Manufacturing Company," January 13, 2000, available at http://www.chemrest.com/domestic%20preparedness.pdf

[152] "Definitions of WMD" Produced by the Monterey Institute's Center for Nonproliferation Studies. Updated January 2006. http://www.nti.org/f_wmd411/f1a1.html

[153] President George W. Bush, "National Strategy to Combat Weapons of Mass Destruction," December 2002. http://www.whitehouse.gov/news/releases/2002/12/WMDStrategy.pdf.

[154] Ibid.

[155] Aaron Klein, "Iran missile transfer puts most Israelis in range" *World Net Daily*, May 30, 2006, at http://www.worldnetdaily.com/news/article.asp?ARTICLE_ID=50427

[156] Ibid.

[157] Examples are from *Public Health Emergency Response Guide* Version 1.0 published by the Department of Health and Human Services, Centers for Disease Control and Prevention, and available at http://www.bt.cdc.gov/planning/pdf/cdcresponseguide.pdf

[158] John D. Negroponte, "Annual Threat Assessment of the Director of National Intelligence for the Senate Select Committee on Intelligence," February 2, 2006, http://www.dni.gov/testimonies/20060202_testimony.pdf

[159] U.S. Department of Homeland Security, *Ready America*, "Clean air," at http://www.ready.gov/america/clean_air.html

[160] *Ready America*, http://www.ready.gov/america/stay_or_go.html

[161] Arturo Casadevall, "Passive antibody administration (immediate immunity) as a specific defense against biological weapons," August 2002, as posted by Department of Health and Human Services Centers for Disease Control and Prevention on "Emerging Infectious Diseases." http://www.cdc.gov/ncidod/EID/vol8no8/01-0516.htm.

[162] Department of Health and Human Services Centers for Disease Control and Prevention Division of Bacterial and Mycotic Diseases, "Anthrax." http://www.cdc.gov/ncidod/dbmd/diseaseinfo/anthrax_g.htm#What%20are%20the%20symptoms%20of%20anthrax.
[163] Ibid.
[164] Department of Health and Human Services Centers for Disease Control and Prevention Division of Bacterial and Mycotic Diseases, "Botulism." http://www.cdc.gov/ncidod/dbmd/diseaseinfo/botulism_g.htm#What%20are%20the%20symptoms%20of%20botulism
[165] Department of Health and Human Services Centers for Disease Control and Prevention Division of Vector-Borne Infectious Diseases, "Plague Fact Sheet." http://www.cdc.gov/ncidod/dvbid/plague/facts.htm
[166] Department of Health and Human Services Centers for Disease Control and Prevention Division of Vector-Borne Infectious Diseases, "Diagnosis." http://www.cdc.gov/ncidod/dvbid/plague/diagnosis.htm
[167] Department of Health and Human Services Centers for Disease Control and Prevention Emergency Preparedness & Response, "Smallpox Fact Sheet." http://www.bt.cdc.gov/agent/smallpox/overview/disease-facts.asp
[168] Department of Health and Human Services Centers for Disease Control and Prevention, Emergency Preparedness & Response, "Key Facts About Tularemia." http://www.bt.cdc.gov/agent/tularemia/facts.asp
[169] Department of Health and Human Services Centers for Disease Control and Prevention, Special Pathogens Branch, "Viral Hemorrhagic Fevers." http://www.cdc.gov/ncidod/dvrd/spb/mnpages/dispages/vhf.htm
[170] http://www.cdc.gov/ncidod/dvrd/spb/mnpages/dispages/vhf.htm
[171] Terrorism Safety Alliance, "Can You Survive a Nuclear Explosion?" http://www.terrorismsafetyalliance.org/Page.asp?PageSubid=15&Pageid=9
[172] "Nuclear Blast" http://www.fema.gov/areyouready/nuclear_blast.shtm Last Modified: Thursday, 23-Mar-2006 20:32:23 EST. Quoted material is in Arial font.
[173] U.S. Department of Health and Human Services Food and Drug Administration Center for Drug Evaluation and Research (CDER), "Potassium Iodide as a Thyroid Blocking Agent in Radiation Emergencies," December 2001. http://www.fda.gov/cder/guidance/4825fnl.htm#Use%20of%20KI%20in%20Radiation%20Emergencies:%20Rationale,%20Effectiveness,%20Safety. Quoted material is in Arial font.
[174] Department of Homeland Security, *Emergency Supply List.* http://www.ready.gov/america/_downloads/checklist.pdf, downloadable from http://www.ready.gov/america/get_a_kit.html.
[175] Federal Emergency Management Agency & American Red Cross, "Food & Water in an Emergency." http://www.redcross.org/static/file_cont39_lang0_24.pdf

[176] Bureau of Diplomatic Security, "Responding to a Biological or Chemical Threat: A Practical Guide," released November 2001, at http://www.state.gov/m/ds/rls/rpt/20214.htm.

[177] John D. Negroponte, "Annual Threat Assessment of the Director of National Intelligence for the Senate Select Committee on Intelligence," February 2, 2006. http://www.dni.gov/testimonies/20060202_testimony.pdf

[178] Since this was written, Zarqawi has been killed.

[179] *Merriam-Webster Online Dictionary.* http://www.merriamwebster.com/dictionary/repent

Printed in the United States
93400LV00008B/67/A